Following
the Money

Following the Money

*The Enron Failure
and the State of
Corporate Disclosure*

George Benston
Michael Bromwich
Robert E. Litan
Alfred Wagenhofer

WITHDRAWN

AEI-BROOKINGS JOINT CENTER
FOR REGULATORY STUDIES
Washington, D.C.

Following the Money may be ordered from:
Brookings Institution Press
1775 Massachusetts Avenue, N.W.
Washington, D.C. 20036
Tel.: (800) 275-1447 or (202) 797-6258
Fax: (202) 797-6004
www.brookings.edu

Library of Congress Cataloging-in-Publication data

Following the money : the Enron failure and the state of corporate
  disclosure / George Benston . . . [et al.].
     p.   cm.
Includes bibliographical references and index.
   ISBN 0-8157-0890-4 (cloth : alk. paper)
     1. Disclosure in accounting—United States.   2. Corporations—United
States—Accounting.   3. Corporations—United States—Auditing.   4.
Accounting—Standards—United States.   5. Financial statements—United
States.   6. Capital market—United States.   7. Enron Corp.—Corrupt
practices.   I. Benston, George J.   II. AEI-Brookings Joint Center for
Regulatory Studies.

HF5658.F65 2003
657'.95'0973—dc21   2003000068

9 8 7 6 5 4 3 2 1

The paper used in this publication meets minimum requirements of the
American National Standard for Information Sciences—Permanence of Paper
for Printed Library Materials: ANSI Z39.48-1984.

Typeset in Adobe Garamond

Composition by
R. Lynn Rivenbark
Macon, Georgia

Printed by
R. R. Donnelley
Harrisonburg, Virginia

Foreword

Only a few short years ago, after the Asian financial crisis of 1997–98, Americans held out their systems of corporate governance and financial disclosure as models to be emulated by the rest of the world. Thomas Friedman, in his best-selling book *The Lexus and the Olive Tree*, cited these features of the U.S. economic system with approval.

It was with some embarrassment then, and no little dismay, that beginning in late 2001 American policymakers and corporate leaders found themselves facing the largest corporate accounting scandals in American history. Although accounting irregularities had shown up in several large corporations in preceding years, they paled in comparison to the abuses uncovered at Enron, WorldCom, and a handful of other American corporate giants. Both Enron and WorldCom went bankrupt. Criminal and civil investigations and lawsuits were pending in those and several other cases as 2002 drew to a close. The scandals led the Bush administration to call for far-reaching reforms in both the corporate governance and financial disclosure regimes. Congress quickly followed by enacting most of them, and others, in the Corporate Responsibility Act of 2002.

Policymakers were not the only ones to take quick action in the wake of the scandals. The major stock exchanges—the New York Stock Exchange and the NASDAQ—made fundamental changes to their listing requirements. The private sector acted as well. Corporate boards of directors and managers now give disclosure issues far more attention and scrutiny than before. Accounting firms—watching in horror as one of their largest, Arthur Andersen, collapsed after a criminal conviction for document shredding—have tightened their auditing procedures. Stock analysts and ratings agencies, hit hard by a series of disclosures about their failings, have changed their practices as well.

As embarrassed and shocked as Americans may have been about these events, they also can be proud that the U.S. political and economic system had enough strength to address the problems almost as soon as they were uncovered. But will these reforms be enough? Are some counterproductive? And are other shortcomings in the disclosure system, both in the United States and elsewhere, still in need of correction or at least serious attention by policymakers?

These are among the questions that George Benston, Michael Bromwich, Robert E. Litan, and Alfred Wagenhofer address in this book. The authors had begun the project that has culminated in this book even before the Enron scandal broke. As they explain, even setting the scandals aside, the corporate disclosure system needs to be updated to reflect changes in the underlying economy and to make full use of new communications and analytical technologies, the Internet in particular. The series of accounting scandals in 2001 and 2002, however, prompted the authors to shift direction and to address specifically the nature of the problems those scandals revealed and the efficacy of the remedies that have since been adopted to address them.

The broad message of this book is that while the various "fixes" should improve matters, some were unnecessary, and some problems remain unaddressed. The authors advance what are sure to be some controversial suggestions: that rather than attempt to craft a single set of accounting and reporting standards for all companies throughout the world, policymakers should allow a competition in standards, at least between the two major sets (Generally Accepted Accounting Principles, or GAAP, in the United States, and International Financial Reporting Standards); that policymakers should encourage experimentation in disclosure of a variety of nonfinancial indicators to better enable investors and analysts to ascertain the source and nature of intangible assets; and that policymakers should exploit the advantages of the Internet by encouraging more frequent financial disclosures in a form that will make them more widely accessible and more easily used.

This book could not come at a better time—when accounting and disclosure issues are now at the top of the public policy agenda and very much on investors' minds. The authors hope that the book will help contribute to better understanding of these issues.

The authors are grateful to a number of individuals who have helped make this project and the book possible: to Sandip Sukhtankar and Chris Lyddy for research assistance; to Dennis Berresford, Robert K. Elliott, Robert Hahn, and Katherine Schipper for comments and suggestions on earlier drafts; to Martha Gottron and Margaret Langston for editorial assistance; to Gloria Paniagua for verification of the manuscript; and to Alicia Jones for secretarial support. The authors remain responsible, however, for the manuscript and its contents, any errors, or omissions.

This book was prepared under the auspices, and with the funding, of the AEI-Brookings Joint Center for Regulatory Studies. The Joint Center builds on the expertise of both sponsoring institutions on regulatory issues. The primary purpose of the Joint Center is to hold lawmakers and regulators accountable for their decisions by providing thoughtful, objective analysis of existing regulatory programs and new regulatory proposals. This book helps carry out this mission with its special focus on rules relating to corporate disclosure and governance.

ROBERT W. HAHN
Director

ROBERT E. LITAN
Codirector

*AEI-Brookings Joint Center
on Regulatory Studies*

Contents

Following
the Money

1 | *The Crisis in*
Corporate Disclosure

Only a few short years ago, the American system of corporate disclosure—the combination of accounting and auditing standards, the professionalism of auditors, and the rules and practices of corporate governance that are designed to ensure the timely dissemination of relevant and accurate corporate financial information—was championed as a model for the rest of the world. In the aftermath of the Asian financial crisis of 1997–98, which was marked by among other things a woeful lack of disclosure by companies, commercial banks, and even central banks, American commentators and experts were urging not only Asian countries, but others as well, to adopt the key features of the U.S. disclosure system.

How much has changed since then! A corporate disclosure system that Americans thought was beyond reproach has turned out to be flawed in ways that few would have imagined or dared suggest only a few years earlier. The shift in attitude is reflected in various measures, among them earnings restatements. The number of American corporations whose earnings have been restated rose modestly throughout the 1990s, but then took a big jump in 1998 and hit a peak of more than 200 in 1999.[1] All the while, concern has continued to mount about "earnings management" by many companies. Under this practice, strongly decried by Arthur Levitt, a recent past chairman of the Securities and Exchange Commission (SEC), firms exploit the discretion allowed under accounting rules to ensure that their earnings show continued growth or at least reach the quarterly earnings estimates put out by financial analysts.

Nothing, however, has done more to generate widespread public and official concern about the usefulness of current disclosures by corporations than the failure of Enron in the fall of 2001 and the subsequent disclosures of misconduct by its auditor, Arthur Andersen. Among other things, Andersen was alleged to have known about the company's problems but did nothing to force Enron to reveal them and may even have helped the company deceive the public. In May 2002, Andersen was convicted of obstruction of justice for shredding key Enron documents. Criminal charges and civil lawsuits are still pending against Enron, Andersen, and some of their top managers.

The Enron-Andersen debacle would have been bad enough, but it was quickly followed by revelations of accounting irregularities at several other leading companies. In late June 2002, the telecommunications giant WorldCom disclosed an earnings restatement approaching $4 billion, which was subsequently revised upward in November 2002 to potentially more than $9 billion. That announcement was followed by one from Xerox disclosing a $1.4 billion restatement. As of the end of August 2002, high-profile lawsuits and official investigations, involving fifteen major companies, had been launched against five leading accounting firms for auditing failure, as shown in table 1-1.

The events relating to Enron, WorldCom, AOL/Time Warner, Xerox, and some of the other companies listed in table 1-1 have had repercussions far beyond the companies involved, their current or former officers and directors, and their auditors. The thousands of employees who once worked for and had their pensions tied to the fortunes of now bankrupt firms have suffered deep economic pain, while investors in these firms collectively have lost billions. The stock markets fell steadily and sharply through much of the spring and into the summer. By the end of July 2002, the S&P 500 Index—one of the broadest gauges of the market—had fallen

Table 1-1. *Major Accounting Investigations or Lawsuits*

Company	Auditor
Adelphia	Deloitte & Touche
AOL/Time Warner	Ernst & Young
Bristol-Meyers-Squibb	PricewaterhouseCoopers
Computer Associates	Ernst & Young
Enron	Arthur Andersen
Global Crossing	Arthur Andersen
Merck	Arthur Andersen
MicroStrategy	PricewaterhouseCoopers
PeopleSoft	Ernst & Young
PNC Financial Services	Ernst & Young
Qwest	Arthur Andersen
Tyco	PricewaterhouseCoopers
Waste Management	Arthur Andersen
WorldCom	Arthur Andersen
Xerox	KPMG

Source: Amy Borrus, Mike McNamee, and Susan Zegel, "Corporate Probes: A Scorecard," *Business Week*, June 10, 2002, pp. 42–43, and subsequent media reports through August 2002.

nearly 30 percent in just three months.[2] The market continued to fall for some time after that, most likely due to jitters over an impending war with Iraq, before beginning to climb again. At this writing, in late fall 2002, the market had recovered, but only to roughly its post-July, depressed level. In any event, the apparent shattering of investor confidence and continued spate of accounting stories pushed Congress into quickly enacting a comprehensive package of measures—the Corporate Responsibility Act of 2002, perhaps better known as the Sarbanes-Oxley Act after its primary sponsors—designed to reform not only corporate accounting but corporate governance more broadly.

The fall of Enron also raised broad concerns about current accounting standards that the Sarbanes-Oxley Act did not specifically address, such as whether the standards are too slow in the making and too heavily influenced by narrow interests. Questions have also been asked about the effectiveness of existing rules and the institutions that are charged with designing and enforcing them—the legal and ethical duties of corporate officers and directors, financial and market regulation, litigation, and self-regulation of the auditing profession. Together these institutions are supposed to ensure that corporate officers and directors, as well as auditors, serve the interests of shareholders. Indeed, the various accounting-related debacles have called into question the efficacy of the entire system of corporate governance in the United States, prompting not only a thorough soul-searching in executive suites, but tougher governance requirements for companies listed on organized exchanges. The situation was summed up in a widely noted speech delivered by Henry M. Paulson, Jr., the chief executive officer of Goldman Sachs, in June 2002: "In my life, American business has never been under such scrutiny. To be blunt, much of it is deserved."[3]

We certainly share the view that the U.S. system of corporate disclosure and governance has problems and is in need of change—it is that view that has prompted us to write this book. But we are concerned that in the rush to assign blame for Enron and the other accounting debacles, policymakers may be overreacting in some areas and taking actions in others that may prove to be ineffective or even counterproductive. We also urge policymakers not to think that they have now done all they can. A combination of forces calls for even more fundamental changes in disclosure practices: the increasing global character of capital markets, the ability of the Internet and new computer languages to speed up and enhance investor access to corporate information, and the rising importance of intangible assets in creating shareholder value for many corporations.

We recognize, of course, that even under the best of circumstances, policy has trouble anticipating constructive change—and for that reason, some think policymakers should not even make the attempt. But at the very least, policy should not fall behind or slow down constructive change. For that reason, the job for policymakers interested in and concerned about the future corporate disclosure remains unfinished.

One word about our expected readership. We suspect that many, if not most, of our readers will be from the United States, where the companies whose books have been questioned are domiciled and where these broad concerns about disclosure have been raised. Understandably, therefore, much of the focus of this book is on the U.S. disclosure system. But as we hope to make clear in this initial chapter, the issues discussed here have much broader significance and import: they affect or should affect thinking throughout the world about the effectiveness of corporate disclosure systems everywhere. One of our modest hopes in writing this book, therefore, is to help others who share this interest and concern to come to grips with the same issues and questions that are, at this writing, very much on the minds of American policymakers and the wider public.

Corporate Disclosure: Why It Matters

Markets of all types require information to function. Buyers must know what sellers are offering. Otherwise transactions are not likely to occur, or if they do, the prices at which they occur will be distorted because buyers are not well informed.

The capital markets are no exception. Lenders certainly must know about the financial details of their borrowers. Moreover, the typical bank loan or bond has a series of covenants, requiring the borrower to continue to meet certain financial tests or face the prospect of higher interest rates or even default.

We concentrate in this book for several reasons on disclosure of information to equities investors, however, and by implication to the equities markets. The overriding reason is that the current system of disclosure—by law and by practice—has developed to satisfy the needs of equities investors in particular. The disclosure system, in turn, rests on the acceptance of a body of accounting standards. In the United States, these standards are set by the Financial Accounting Standards Board (FASB), which derives its authority from the Securities and Exchange Commission (SEC), the regulatory body charged with protecting investors in corporations with publicly traded shares.[4] Elsewhere around the world, nations increasingly are accepting International Financial Reporting Standards (IFRS), set by the International Accounting Standards Board (IASB).

We focus here on equities investors for another reason: because they are growing more numerous, not only in the United States but elsewhere. In the United States, the share of households investing in stock directly or through mutual funds rose from 32 percent in 1989 to more than 50 percent in 2001. Excluding pension fund holdings, equities have also climbed sharply as a share of household financial assets: from a low of

Table 1-2. *Equity Ownership in Selected Countries*

Country	Initial share or number	Later share or number	Definition
Canada[a]	23% (1989)	49% (2000)	Share of adults who own directly or indirectly
China[b]	11 million (1995)	55 million (2000)	Number of investors
Germany[c]	3.5% (1998)	7% (1999)	Share of adults who own directly or indirectly
Japan[d]	14% (1989)	5% (late 1990s)	Equity ownership of individual investors
Korea[e]	2–3 million (1990)	7–8 million (2000)	Number of investors
Norway[f]	14% (1994)	17% (1998)	Direct or indirect ownership

a. *Canadian Shareowners Study 2000,* conducted by Market Probe Canada on behalf of the Toronto Stock Exchange (www.tse.com/news/monthly_22.html).

b. David R. Francis, "The Rise of a Global 'Shareholder Culture,'" *Christian Science Monitor,* July 2000, p. 14 (www.csmonitor.com/durable/2000/07/03/p14s2.htm).

c. "Go Global," *Kiplinger's Personal Finance,* May 2000 (www.kiplinger.com/magazine/archives/2000/May/investing/global1.htm).

d. "Japan's Missed Opportunity," *The Globalist,* June 2001.

e. Francis, "The Rise of a Global 'Shareholder Culture.'"

f. Steven T. Goldberg, "Stock Markets Win the Masses," *Christian Science Monitor,* March 1998 (www.csmonitor.com/durable/1998/03/25/intl/intl.7.htm).

11 percent in 1982 to a high of 46 percent in the first quarter of 2000, before falling back to 33 percent in the third quarter of 2001.[5] Table 1-2 illustrates that stock ownership has also risen in other countries. The increase in and relative amount of equity ownership in Canada look very much like that in the United States. However, stock ownership in Europe and Japan still lags the United States significantly.

Equities investors, or at least the industry of analysts and brokers who advise them, are interested in information that enables them to project future cash flows of the companies in which they hold stock. That is because, in principle, the value of a share of stock is simply the present discounted value of future dividends, which are derived from estimated cash flows. Accounting information contained in income and funds flow statements and balance sheets, while backward-looking by definition, is nonetheless a critical input in most attempts to project future performance of firms. To the extent the market deems accounting information unreliable, investors confront "information risk" in making investment decisions. The higher the information risks, the less attractive are stocks in comparison with alternative investments. Higher information risk thus depresses stock prices.

Furthermore, equity holders as well as creditors have reason to be concerned about the validity of the numbers presented in financial reports. They cannot personally examine the books and accounts of corporations. Nor can they determine that corporate assets have not been misappropriated, liabilities understated, or net income falsified.

In short, investors have a very real interest in the information that corporations disclose, the trustworthiness of the disclosure, and how and when they disclose it. The Enron affair and the other accounting episodes have cast a pall over U.S. equities, and until confidence in the numbers returns, that pall is not likely to be completely lifted.

Defining the Problem

We begin our analysis in chapter 2, where we offer our view of what is wrong with the current system of financial statement disclosure in the United States. We use the Enron case as a point of departure, but also generalize from prior events and trends. In brief, we argue that the major problem revealed by Enron and other recent accounting scandals lies not so much in the accounting and auditing standards themselves as in the system of *enforcing* those standards. The legal system and its threat of criminal and civil liability will no doubt prove to be very real when the Enron and Arthur Andersen litigation is over. But somewhat surprisingly, the possibility of being held liable for their actions did not deter bad conduct by Enron's management, its directors, and its auditors. Nor has the legal system, even the threat of criminal liability for those engaging in misconduct, deterred accounting abuses in the other instances summarized earlier in table 1-1.

We do not mean to say that current accounting standards are perfect. In chapter 2, we point out that one major initiative of the FASB and its international counterpart, the IASB—the move toward "fair-value" accounting—is misplaced. Fair values are not always market values, that is, values based on arm's-length reliable market transactions. Rather, fair values for assets not regularly traded in public markets must be calculated from corporate managers' estimates of the present values of expected cash flows. These numbers often are very difficult to determine and even more difficult for auditors to verify. In fact, Enron used fair-value accounting to report income of doubtful validity, thereby giving the appearance of superior performance that, in fact, did not exist. If accounting standard setters want to reduce the likelihood of future Enrons, they should abandon current efforts to rely further on fair values for financial reports (although we do not object to the use of fair values as *supplements* to required financial reports where they can be reliably determined and independently verified). This is perhaps one of the more important and less publicized lessons for accounting standards of the Enron failure.

In contrast, we believe too much attention has been paid during the entire Enron episode to the accounting rules governing the many "special purpose entities" (SPEs) that Enron created. Much of the reporting in the media suggested that the Enron problem arose because the then-current rules governing accounting for SPEs were too weak in that they did not require Enron to consolidate the assets and liabilities of these off-balance-sheet entities with those of the company itself. But publicly available evidence on the Enron case neither proves that allegation nor refutes it. The essential problem was Enron's failure to follow the requirement to disclose, in footnote form, the amount and other relevant details about the SPEs' debt for which Enron was liable and, only in certain cases, to fully reflect the losses suffered by the SPEs in Enron's own income statement. Consequently, the Enron case does not justify one way or the other the FASB's subsequent proposal to reform SPE consolidation rules.[6]

There are larger problems with the process by which accounting standards are developed, however. Because the FASB has been given the functional equivalent of a monopoly in standard setting, it is not surprising that its rule development is slow to respond to market developments. Moreover, although the FASB is a technically independent body, it effectively reports to the SEC, which in turn reports to Congress. As a result, on occasion politics and demands by politically powerful groups, rather than substance, have strongly influenced the FASB's rulemaking process—the highest-profile examples being the accounting treatment for stock options and oil and gas accounting.

Fixing the Problems

Chapter 3 outlines what we believe to be prudent solutions to the problems identified in chapter 2. The "fix" for the movement toward fair-value accounting, on the surface, would appear to be an easy one: just stop it and require that all numbers presented in financial statements be reliable and that external auditors be held to their responsibility to inform investors that the numbers follow the dictates of the accounting standards, however specified.

The solutions to the more generic problems with the FASB's rulemaking are inherently more difficult to fashion. For example, it has been suggested that all could be resolved if U.S. accounting standards, known as Generally Accepted Accounting Principles (GAAP), simply were replaced with the international standards developed by the IASB. To be sure, an organization based in London that sets standards followed by many countries might be less prone to political influence, at least from narrowly drawn groups in the United States. But politics may surface in a different form in the international arena. Furthermore, an international accounting body with representatives from many different countries is as likely to become bogged down over time in developing new rules, as is now the case with the FASB in the United States.

An alternative is for the two major standard-setting bodies to harmonize differences between the two sets of standards in an effort to develop a single set meant to apply worldwide. In fact, the IASB and the FASB launched such an effort in September 2002, with the aim of eliminating all major differences between the two sets of standards by 2005. However, for reasons we lay out in later portions of this book, this is an extremely ambitious undertaking and one whose successful outcome over the long run is hardly assured.

Competition among Standards

We therefore believe instead that a more promising approach for shortening any delay in rulemaking and for reducing undue political influence is to allow some form of *competition* in standard setting. We consider a range of options in chapter 3:

—*controlled competition,* under which companies listing their shares, regardless of their country of domicile, would be allowed to choose between the U.S. standards and IASB standards, *without reconciling the differences attributed to the use of one standard rather than the other;*[7]

—*constrained competition,* under which companies would be allowed the same choice as under controlled competition, but only after the FASB and the IASB have narrowed some of the key differences between the two sets of standards (such as the rules relating to consolidation and stock options);

—*limited competition,* under which companies could choose between the two standards, but would be required to reconcile "material" differences between them; and

—*mutual recognition,* in which the FASB and the IASB each would maintain their monopoly rulemaking authority in their localities, but the U.S. authorities in particular would recognize foreign-domiciled companies' use of the IASB standards (while still requiring U.S. companies to report under U.S. standards).

Of these options, we prefer the first on theoretical grounds but recognize that it has the lowest likelihood of adoption. The constrained competition option is less ambitious than the harmonization effort between the IASB and the FASB now under way and may be more feasible. The same may be true of the limited competition option. Either of these options, however, would generate less benefit from competition. Mutual recognition of accounting standards would produce the fewest competitive benefits, because it would leave undisturbed the local monopoly power of the two standard-setting organizations.

In outlining possible forms of standards competition, we concentrate our attention on IFRS and U.S. GAAP for practical reasons. There is a growing movement worldwide toward the adoption of IFRS as the single standard. Indeed, the European Commission already has required all companies listing their shares on European exchanges to use only IFRS by 2005. That leaves U.S. GAAP as the only real practical alternative to IFRS (unless the two standards are harmonized and encouraged to converge, which is the current policy of the two standard setters).

We also recognize that a competition in standards of some type could sacrifice some comparability, and perhaps transparency, for the benefits of competition. The clear virtue of having a single standard in any jurisdiction is that it eliminates the need for users to learn and apply several different standards. Indeed, the fact that financial markets have become more global in character—whether measured by financial flows across borders, holdings of foreign stocks, or listings by foreign companies on exchanges in different countries—would seem to strengthen the case for a single set of reporting standards that would apply worldwide.

But the costs of allowing multiple standards can be overstated. We strongly suspect, and indeed expect, that if competition were allowed, third-party analysts would provide some sort of company-by-company reconciliation for investors as a way of demonstrating their value as analysts. Such reconciliations are already required by the SEC for foreign companies using IFRS (or any accounting standard other than U.S. GAAP) that want to list their shares on U.S. exchanges. These reconciliations necessarily will be limited if companies reporting under one standard do not disclose as much information as they would if required to prepare any reconciliation. Nonetheless, market pressure might cause companies to provide a similar level of information for reconciliation purposes as is the case under a mandatory system. Alternatively, approximate reconciliations performed by third parties might be more than adequate for investors to make informed decisions, including a decision to forbear from investing because the available information is inadequate.

The benefits of a single set of world standards also can be exaggerated. As it is now, investors rarely can make true "apples-to-apples" comparisons of financial statements of companies that use the same set of accounting principles. For example, many important accounting numbers do not reflect economic values and can be accounted for and reported in different ways; examples are depreciation and the reported figures for the many assets that are not regularly traded at prices determined at arm's-length in active markets. Companies that group activities in ways that are most meaningful to their operations may, as a consequence, report figures that are not comparable with those of other companies. Many accounting rules are based on judgments, such as the useful economic lives of buildings and equipment and the amount of future employment benefits. Judgments on such matters, no matter how reasonable, are likely to differ. Additionally, managers cannot be prevented from manipulating important numbers reported in financial statements by advancing or delaying expenditures and sales. Hence, adoption of a single accounting standard worldwide still would not allow analysts to make apples-to-apples comparisons.

Furthermore, any single set of standards announced by an international body, such as the IASB, is unlikely to retain its monopoly status for long. Precisely because the international standards have been crafted by IASB in more general terms than the U.S. standards, leaving more discretion with professional accountants and firms, standard setters in different countries may issue their own interpretive rulings. Over time, this process would lead to a fragmentation of the single standard and thus back to the current situation, or at least to a coexistence of two sets of standards, the international set and the country-specific set.

In short, the search for a single set of accounting standards is akin to the desire of some to have only one language spoken and written throughout the world. Readers of the Bible know the outcome of that quest. We suspect a similar, although not identical, outcome in the search for a common set of accounting or reporting standards.

Enforcement

What about fixing the enforcement problems exposed by Enron and the other investigations of accounting irregularities listed in table 1-1? In the summer of 2002, the U.S. Congress created a new body, the Public Company Accounting Oversight Board, which reports to the SEC, to oversee and discipline the auditing profession—a task that had been a responsibility of the SEC itself. Much controversy quickly followed over who was going to be selected to chair this oversight body and whether it would have "real teeth." We believe that the creation of this agency and the debate over its chairman were largely a sideshow. Admittedly, there is a need for stronger oversight of auditors, but we fail to see why the job must be handed off to yet another agency. Any past failure on the part of the SEC to discipline individual auditors (or their firms) who were negligent (or perhaps worse) in performing their audits could easily have been cured by providing the SEC with greater resources and statutory authority to impose more calibrated penalties, such as fines. (During the summer of 2002, Congress initially appeared ready to give the SEC additional resources, but then failed to follow through after the administration curiously backed a much lower appropriation increase than Congress was considering.) In any event, the key point, in our view, is that there was, and remains, no need to have delegated the enforcement function to yet another body.

Furthermore, there are limits to how much any oversight body—be it the newly created board or the SEC—can accomplish. Just as the presence of the police and a judicial system have not stamped out crime, the best of audit watchdogs will not eliminate all auditor negligence or wrongdoing. The challenge for policy is to supplement oversight with appropriate *incentives* for auditors to carry out their duties properly, so that after-the-fact investigation and punishment is less necessary.

In principle, the prospect of liability for damages should be a sufficient incentive for accounting firms to perform faithfully; indeed, the likelihood that it will incur heavy legal damages probably would have been the undoing of Arthur Andersen even if the firm had not been convicted of document shredding. But liability law—and the threat of financially debilitating damages—can be too blunt an instrument. A more finely calibrated approach toward incentives is called for.

One obvious place to start is by ensuring that firms and their auditors have appropriate incentives to perform careful audits from the start. The Sarbanes-Oxley Act of 2002 appropriately requires that only the audit committees of boards of directors, rather than the corporate managers, may hire and fire external auditors and that the audit committee be composed only of independent directors. We disagree, however, with another "solution" to the incentives problem included in that law: prohibiting auditing firms from performing nonaudit work for their corporate clients.[8] Auditors who might be suborned by the prospect of gaining or fear of losing consulting fees are just as likely to be suborned by similar concerns about audit fees. The result of this prohibition, we fear, is higher audit fees and less effective audits, costs that necessarily will be borne by shareholders.

Many of the recent changes in U.S. law governing auditing are likely to be beneficial, primarily because they establish a potentially more effective system for enforcing adherence to accounting standards by individual public accountants and accounting firms. But the problem of enforcing standards internationally still remains. For securities markets to be effective vehicles for investment worldwide, investors must be able to trust and understand corporate financial statements worldwide. Currently, there is no global system of enforcement of accounting and auditing standards.

We do not believe the leading nations of the world are ready to give an official multilateral institution, such as the International Organization of Securities Commissions (IOSCO), sufficient enforcement powers over auditors to be a meaningful watchdog. During the past several years, the world's top accounting firms, under the auspices of the International Federation of Accountants, have been working on a different approach: international self-regulation. Quite clearly, in the wake of Enron and the other U.S. accounting scandals, such a suggestion may seem counterintuitive. But, as we argue in chapter 3, no other practical alternative currently exists. Given the embarrassment of self-regulation in the United States, there is at least a chance that the major accounting firms would want the opportunity to redeem themselves on the world stage. That effort should therefore be supported, at least for now.

Looking Ahead

As important as the issues and problems immediately exposed by the various U.S. accounting debacles may be, a number of more fundamental developments affecting capital markets call for new thinking about overall corporate disclosure policies and practices. We identify and briefly discuss several of these factors in our concluding chapter.

The first major trend affecting disclosure practices is the increased use of the Internet, which enables companies to provide information almost instantly to all interested investors simultaneously. In principle, this ability should make securities markets even more efficient.

A related trend is the development of a common financial language designed for the Internet, XBRL, which will assign "tags" to all kinds of financial and other data reported by companies for various purposes. Provided that commonly accepted definitions for different types of information can be agreed on—and this process appears to be well under way—these tags not only may become widely used inside companies for organizing data and between companies for completing transactions, but they could help transform the way financial statements and other reports are presented to the public.

One caveat to this futuristic view, however, is worth noting. Although technologies and standards governing the identification of accounts, such as XBRL, are likely to be very useful for investors and analysts, they do not eliminate the demand by investors for *reliable* information across firms and countries. Audits will still be needed to assure users that companies are identifying their accounts in accordance with an XBRL manual and the definitions of the various tags. Auditing and enforcement therefore will remain important, whether or not there is agreement on rules governing the specific presentation of information. Indeed, until any additional nonfinancial information is subject to some type of auditing process, it will in some fundamental sense be less reliable than the audited financial data.

Nonetheless, nonfinancial information at the same time may become as important, if not more important, to projecting future earnings growth and thus to stock price valuation, than currently reported financial information. This possibility grows out of a second key trend that should affect corporate disclosure: the growing importance of intangible assets to the creation of shareholder wealth. Intangible assets range from intellectual property such as patents and trade secrets to the value of a company's brand, its work force and customer base—in short, all items that contribute to a company's ability to generate revenue but that generally cannot be bought and sold in the marketplace independent of the company itself.

Some observers have responded to the increased importance of intangible assets by proposing development of standards for recording such assets on balance sheets, whether the assets were purchased or developed inhouse. We reject this approach largely because most intangibles are not bought and sold on the open market and thus have no reliable market value; requiring a value to be assigned to these assets would subject the reported numbers to opportunistic manipulation. Instead, we recommend that securities regulators encourage companies to experiment with the release of various kinds of nonfinancial information and let the market sort out which sorts of disclosures investors value most. At the same time, it would behoove regulators or standard setters to begin thinking hard about what, if any, features of these new experiments in nonfinancial disclosures ought to be mandated (as some countries such as the United Kingdom are beginning to do), and the extent to which independent public accountants should attest to their trustworthiness.

Finally, what role will analysts play in the future, or perhaps more accurately, what role should they play? In the wake of the various accounting scandals, several major investment banks were investigated by state and federal authorities for allowing, indeed encouraging, their research analysts to "hype" the shares of companies the banks marketed. Other abuses, such as selective handouts of shares of initial public offerings to executives of other major clients, were also investigated. After a flurry of interest in forcing the investment banks to divest their research operations, the likely reforms became more moderate: the erection of new forms of firewalls between investment banks and sell-side analysts, and changes in the compensation of the analysts.

As interesting as the debate over the future of investment bank analysts has become, we believe its importance will fade over the long run as new technologies, such as XBRL, lower barriers to entry in the analyst industry. In the process, the industry should become more competitive, assuming sufficient investor demand exists to support analysts independent of brokerage or other investment banking activities. At a minimum, the new technology will make it easier for buy-side analysts working for institutional investors to do their jobs, while also empowering increasing numbers of individual investors to do their own research and stock-picking. The net result may well be a shift away from, or at least a slowdown in the growth of, index investing that has become so popular over the past several decades.

Conclusion

For those interested in the subject of corporate disclosure, these are interesting, indeed exciting, times. But not by choice. The scandals surrounding the disclosure failures and shortcomings associated with Enron, WorldCom, and a handful of other large public companies have focused public attention on accounting and disclosure policies in a way many may never have imagined and few welcomed.

The challenge now for policymakers is to make corrections without damaging the disclosure process. We outline in this book what we believe is a prudent agenda for achieving this objective. We hope readers will agree, or at least recognize that the issues relating to corporate disclosure are more interesting and more complicated than they may have realized.

2 | *What's Wrong—and Right— with Corporate Accounting and Auditing in the United States*

Criticism of corporate accounting is not new. Strident complaints about dishonest and deceptive accounting in the 1920s[1] and the distress of the Great Depression led to the creation in 1933 of the Securities and Exchange Commission. The SEC was given the authority to prescribe, monitor, and enforce accounting rules that presumably would help investors make informed decisions. The SEC quickly delegated its rulemaking function, first to the American Institute of Certified Public Accountants (AICPA) in 1936, and then in 1973 to the Financial Accounting Standards Board, but the commission remained responsible for monitoring and enforcing accounting standards.

The Enron affair and the other recent accounting scandals demonstrate only too well that accounting problems remain. But before "fixes" are made, it is essential to know what exactly is wrong with accounting—and with corporate disclosure more broadly.

We begin by describing the major purposes and limitations of accounting information—specifically the numbers embodied in financial statements. To instill and maintain investor confidence, such information must be *trustworthy.* That in turn requires

—that the financial figures be reported according to a *well-accepted convention* (Generally Accepted Accounting Principles, or GAAP);

—that the figures be *reliable,* in that they are verified by an independent accounting expert with data derived from relevant market transactions, in accordance with a well-accepted convention (Generally Accepted Auditing Standards, or GAAS); and

—that the reporting and auditing conventions be effectively *enforced* by market forces or an appropriate government or industry agency.

We then argue that the common element in the Enron and the other recent accounting scandals was not a major flaw in the standards themselves, but primarily *a failure either of the company to comply with the standards or of the regulator to enforce them.* Indeed, what was perhaps most surprising about the entire Enron affair is how the many so-called "gatekeeping" institutions set up to ensure proper disclosure all failed to do their jobs. These gatekeeping mechanisms include effective and timely guidance on accounting standards by the FASB and the SEC; fiduciary responsibilities imposed on management and directors; auditors; regulators of the accounting profession (state and federal, and the AICPA); and the threat of legal liability.

The Enron case has exposed, however, a major trend in accounting standards both in the United States and at the international level—a movement toward "fair-value accounting"—that we believe is disturbing and inconsistent with the reliability objective of good accounting standards. This issue has received relatively little attention among analysts, and we intend to give it more in this chapter. The standards issue that has received much greater public attention—appropriate accounting for special purpose entities—is of secondary concern, or at least is not resolved one way or the other by the Enron episode. Enron's other major failing was inadequate reporting of and accounting for a conflict of interest accepted by its board of directors.

In short, the Enron affair does not, in our view, justify a full-scale assault on current accounting standards. Nonetheless, for reasons that predated Enron and that continue to be valid, those standards do have their limitations.

Furthermore, the *standard-setting process* in the United States has several major flaws, in our view. We identify these at the end of this chapter and propose possible solutions in chapter 3.

The Value of Audited Financial Statements to Shareholders

The securities laws in the United States were established largely to ensure that investors have as much information as they need, and when they need it, to make informed decisions about whether to buy, hold, or sell shares in publicly traded and widely held corporations. Accordingly, it is something of conventional wisdom that disclosure serves the interests of investors. But why?

Most prospective investors realize that once they have committed their funds to a corporation, either by purchasing shares directly or from a shareholder, they will have little control over how the corporation is managed. Consequently, they usually are interested in how those who do have control use corporate resources, and the extent to which controlling persons (including senior managers) have conflicts of interest that might result in costs being imposed on noncontrolling shareholders. Reporting in these areas is called the "stewardship" function of accounting. Financial reports also help to motivate managers to operate their corporations in the interest of shareholders. This is called the "agency" or "contracting" function of accounting.

In addition to information on stewardship, investors want data that help them determine the present and possible future economic value of their investments. If the corporation's shares are actively traded in a market, shareholders can obtain seemingly unbiased estimates of the economic value of their investments from share prices. But these prices are based, in part, on the information provided in financial reports. If this information is not useful and reliable, its receipt will not provide investors with insights that they want. Prospective investors then might have to incur costs to obtain information elsewhere or discount the amount they are willing to pay for the shares, using the information currently available to them. This would make the shares worth less to them, and they would pay less for them, to the detriment of current shareholders.

Trust Is the Key to Accounting Information

In short, shareholders, including those who can exercise some control over the corporation, benefit when corporate managers provide all investors with financial reports that investors find *trustworthy*. We believe that at least three characteristics ensure trustworthiness. First, financial reports are likely to be trustworthy if they are prepared according to a *well-accepted set of conventions*, or accounting standards. In principle, standards should reduce the costs to investors of understanding and evaluating the condition, performance, and prospects of companies and of comparing financial reports from different companies. Standards thus enhance the demand for shares generally. Standards also can help protect the independent professional accountants, or "external auditors," who help enforce them, as we note shortly. Because in the past external auditors were generally hired and fired by managers,[2] codified accounting concepts and standards and auditing procedures could guide external auditors and protect them from demands by clients to attest to numbers that might mislead users of financial statements. External auditors could rightly claim that there was no point for the client to go to another auditor who might be more compliant, because all auditors were supposed to adhere to the standards.

In the United States, the FASB sets Generally Accepted Accounting Principles (GAAP), although it can be and, on occasion, has been overruled by the SEC. Generally Accepted Auditing Standards (GAAS), meanwhile, are set by the AICPA.[3] For many other countries, particularly those in Europe, accounting standards are codified by the International Accounting Standards Board (IASB), which is headquartered in London. Many individual countries also have their own accounting standards boards and independent accounting associations that establish domestic accounting and auditing standards.

Second, the numbers must be *reliable*, in the sense that they can be verified and replicated and are based on amounts derived from relevant market transactions, where these are available. When market values are not available or reliable, prevailing rules generally do not allow revenues to be estimated because of concern that overly optimistic or opportunistic managers, who are responsible for preparing the estimates, would tend to overstate revenue.[4] However, estimates typically are permitted for expenses, when necessary, because estimates are preferable to not reporting any expenses related to a specific time period or to revenue that is recognized.[5] In addition, predetermined rules are used to record accruals, allocations of revenue, and expenses to specific time periods when the amounts are received or expended in advance of the service to be performed. Of course, reliability is reduced in all cases where it may be appropriate to use estimates, rather than collections of actual transactions data. The critical factor is how much discretion firms and their managers are able to exercise that could potentially mislead investors and other users of financial statements.

Relevance—the capacity of the reported number to influence decisions—is considered by some to be an equally desirable or even more important attribute of accounting than reliability. After all, its proponents point out, the amount paid for a building several years ago may be accurately reported, but it is irrelevant to the current value of the building. It is the value of the building today that investors need to know when they are deciding whether to buy, hold, or sell the stock of the corporation that owns the building. But even if the value of the building could be measured more currently, it still may not be a very relevant measure. At best all that can be reported is the value of the building as of the date of the financial statement, which cannot be the investor's decision date. Worse yet, the values of most assets cannot be determined from the market prices derived from actual transactions of similar assets, because most assets are not regularly traded; and even if these values could be obtained, the value of productive assets to the owners of going concerns (value in use) necessarily exceeds their market values (value in exchange), or the firms would not have purchased the assets.[6] Value in use is the present value of net cash flows expected to be obtained from an asset used by a firm in conjunction with its other operations. These values often are costly to measure, must necessarily be derived from a range of assumptions and estimates, and thus are subject to managerial manipulation.

We conclude, therefore, that estimated values-in-use figures are not actually relevant to investors. Rather, the relevant numbers are those that investors can trust to be what they purport to be: market values, when these are available, or values based on historical cost, adjusted and allocated in accordance with known rules of accounting.[7]

Third, both accounting and auditing standards must be *enforced*. External auditors are supposed to ensure that their audits are conducted in accordance with GAAS and that the financial figures are prepared in accordance with GAAP. An important aspect of the audit is examination and testing of the company's accounting and internal control systems. Who ensures that the auditors are complying with GAAS? Until very recently, audit standards were enforced by the AICPA, state regulators, and the SEC, which can bar an accounting firm found guilty of malfeasance from attesting to the financial statements of public companies in the future. In 2002 Congress gave the SEC's enforcement responsibility over the auditing profession to the newly created Public Company Accounting Oversight Board, which reports to the SEC. In addition, external auditors are or should be disciplined by the threat of loss of their reputations and lawsuits by aggrieved users of financial statements.

What Went Wrong at Enron

Enron's bankruptcy has generated the greatest concern about inadequacies of GAAS and GAAP, in part because for a brief time it was the largest corporate failure in American history (WorldCom's bankruptcy swiftly eclipsed Enron's), and also because of the suddenness of the company's fall from grace.[8] In addition, the Enron case aroused much interest because of the apparent complexity of its operations—initially gas pipelines and later the development and trading of various energy-related financial instruments—and the accounting for these activities.

Enron's stock price increased from a low of about $7 a share in the early 1990s to a high of $90 a share in mid-2000. But on October 16, 2001, the company announced it was reducing its third-quarter, after-tax net income by $1.0 billion and its shareholders' equity by $1.2 billion. On November 8 Enron announced that because of accounting errors, it was restating its previously reported net income for the years 1997 through 2000, cutting stockholders' equity by another $508 million.[9]

In short, within a month, Enron reported stockholders' equity dropping by $1.7 billion, or nearly 20 percent of its $9.6 billion reported value on September 30, 2001. On December 2, 2001, Enron filed for bankruptcy. By the end of 2001, shares of Enron stock were selling for less than $1. Not only did investors and employees whose retirement plans included large amounts of Enron stock lose wealth, but the company's long-time auditor, Arthur Andersen, was later destroyed and the U.S. system of regulating financial accounting came under severe question, with strong and insistent calls for reform.

So what went wrong? Were accounting and auditing standards not up to the job? Or did Enron and its auditor fail to follow the rules that were already in place? Certainly, over time, the congressional, SEC, and other investigations and lawsuits against Enron's officers and directors, accountants, and lawyers will shed increasing light that will help answer these questions. However, a reasonably clear picture of what happened can be painted from information already in the public domain, especially the "Powers Report," released by a special committee of Enron directors on February 1, 2002, following a three-month investigation.[10]

Five types of failures are most noteworthy:

—Enron's failure to account properly for and disclose investments in special purpose entities (SPEs), Enron's contingent liability for their debt, and Enron's dealings with them;

—Enron's incorrect recognition of revenue that increased its reported net income;

—Restatements of merchant investments using fair-value accounting based on unreliable information to overstate both assets and net income of merchant investments;

—Enron's incorrect accounting for its own stock that was issued to and held by SPEs; and

—Inadequate disclosure of and accounting for related-party transactions, conflicts of interest, and their costs to stockholders.

Significantly, all but one of these failures involved violations of the provisions of U.S. GAAP and GAAS. The third failure—relating to Enron's all-too-easy exploitation of the rules relating to fair-value accounting—exposed a real flaw in the current U.S. accounting standards. We now consider each of the failures in somewhat greater detail.

Special Purpose Entities

Many of Enron's accounting misstatements were related to or associated with the company's use of SPEs. Special purpose entities are independently owned enterprises created for a limited purpose, with a limited life and limited activities. SPEs are not unusual; corporations have used them for many years.[11] In particular, banks and financial enterprises used SPEs extensively in the late 1970s and early 1980s to monetize, through off-balance-sheet securitizations, the substantial amounts of consumer receivables on their balance sheets. To our knowledge, very few problems have been associated with financial companies' use of SPEs and guarantees of their debt. That is because the potential losses of these entities have tended to be reliably measured, making it unlikely that the sponsoring companies would have to make good on their debt guarantees. SPEs also have been used by nonfinancial companies to acquire plants and equipment under long-term lease contracts or to fund research and development.

A key question surrounding SPEs raised by the Enron affair is whether and under what circumstances their assets and liabilities should be consolidated with those of their sponsor. Under U.S. GAAP, sponsoring companies are required to consolidate only if they own a majority of the SPE shares or the equity put up by outside investors amounts to less than 3 percent of the SPE's assets.[12] Applied to lease and R&D costs in particular, U.S. GAAP does not require consolidation as long as the sponsoring corporation can demonstrate that the financial risks have been transferred to the SPEs' equity holders.

SPEs have become the financial equivalent of a four-letter word, however, because of Enron's failure and the disclosure that it sponsored hundreds (perhaps thousands) of SPEs with which it did business. Enron used many of these entities to shelter foreign-derived income from U.S. taxes. The SPEs for which its accounting has been criticized, though, were domestic and were created to give Enron a means to avoid reporting losses on some substantial investments. The structure and activities of the specific SPEs in question are quite complicated, in part because the SPEs themselves created other SPEs that dealt with Enron. We present and discuss here only their essential features.[13]

Typically, outside investors held all of the equity in the SPEs, usually amounting to no more than the minimum 3 percent of assets necessary to avoid consolidation. The balance of the financing was provided either through bank loans, guaranteed directly or indirectly by Enron or its subsidiaries, or with restricted Enron stock and options to buy Enron stock at less than market value, for which Enron recorded a note receivable from the SPE. Had Enron accounted for transactions with these SPEs in accordance with GAAP requirements on dealings with related enterprises and disclosure of contingent liabilities for financial guarantees, the company's decision not to consolidate its SPEs as such should not have been an issue.

By our count, however, six accounting problems were associated with Enron's SPEs, *all of which appear to have involved violations of GAAP as it existed at the time.* First, in some important instances, the minimum 3 percent rule was violated, but the affected SPEs were not consolidated. When Andersen realized this failure, it required Enron to restate its financial statements. Second, Enron failed to follow the FASB rule to report clearly in a footnote the amount of financial contingencies for which it was liable as a result of its guarantee of the SPEs' debt.[14] Had this been done, analysts and other users of Enron's statements would have been warned that the corporation could be (and eventually was) liable for a very large amount of debt.

Third, Enron did not consolidate, as it should have, the assets and liabilities of those SPEs that were managed by Enron's chief financial officer, Andrew Fastow, or other employees, and thus effectively controlled by Enron. Fourth, although Enron controlled some SPEs through Fastow, transactions with those SPEs were treated as if they were independent enterprises; as a result net profits on these transactions were improperly recorded on Enron's books. Fifth, Enron funded some SPEs with its own stock or in-the-money options (those with an exercise price below the current stock price) on that stock, taking notes receivable in return. This practice violates a basic accounting procedure, under which companies are prohibited from recording an increase in stockholders' equity unless the stock issued was paid for in cash or its equivalent. Reversal of this error resulted in the $1.2 billion reduction in shareholders' equity in October 2001.

Sixth, Enron used a put option written by an SPE to avoid having to record a loss in value of previously appreciated stock when its market price declined, without disclosing that the option was secured by the SPE's holding of unpaid-for Enron stock and loans guaranteed by Enron. When Enron's investment in the stock declined in value, the SPE could not compensate Enron as promised, because the SPE's assets also declined in value as the price of Enron's stock declined. The SPE also could not pay its bank loans, which shifted the liability to its guarantor, Enron.

In short, Enron's use of SPEs does not demonstrate that the 3 percent-of-equity requirement of U.S. GAAP (for consolidation) was too low, as many have assumed or alleged. Instead, the company engaged in a series of practices with respect to its SPEs that violated the current rules and other accepted accounting principles. Enron abused the current rules and its auditor failed to catch and stop the abuses. That is the lesson one should draw from Enron and its SPEs.

Incorrect Income Recognition

Several of the SPEs paid Enron fees for guarantees on loans made by the SPEs. Although GAAP requires recognition of revenue only over the period of the guarantees, Enron recorded millions of dollars of up-front payments as current revenue. The company also appears to have engineered several sizable "sham sales," where the buyers simultaneously or after a prearranged delay sold back to Enron the same or similar assets at close to the prices they "paid." These dealings wrongly allowed Enron to report profits on the sales and, almost simultaneously, increase the book value of some assets.

Fair-Value Restatements

GAAP requires companies to revalue marketable securities that are not held to maturity to fair values—a term we discuss more extensively later in the chapter—even when these values are not determined from arm's-length market transactions. In such instances, GAAP allows the values to be based on independent appraisals and on models using discounted expected cash flows.

The problem with such models generally is that they allow managers to manipulate net income by making "reasonable" assumptions that give them the gains they want to record. This appears to be what Enron did

with its energy contracts (some of which stretched over ten years) and merchant investments. Particularly egregious is Enron's broadband investment
and joint venture with Blockbuster, Inc., Braveheart. Enron invested more
than $1 billion in broadband and reported revenue of $408 million in
2000, much of it from sales to Fastow-controlled SPEs. In 2000 Enron also
assigned a fair value of $125 million to its Braveheart investment and a
profit of $53 million, even though the venture was only two weeks old and
had not generated any profit. Enron recorded additional revenue of
$53 million from the venture in the first quarter of 2001, although
Blockbuster did not record any income from the venture and dissolved the
partnership in March 2001. In October Enron had to reverse the
$106 million profit it had earlier claimed plus additional losses, a total of
$180 million, an action that contributed to its loss of public trust and sub-
sequent bankruptcy.

As discussed later in the chapter, we believe that fair-value accounting is
inherently subject to the kind of abuses revealed by Enron. We respect
those who maintain instead that Enron abused a set of rules relating to fair
value that can and should be properly enforced. We simply disagree.
Allowing or requiring fair value across the board, especially where there are
no well-developed asset markets to permit verification of valuations, creates
too much opportunity for abuse that we do not believe can be held in
check. We therefore believe that of all the accounting misdeeds relating to
Enron, its abuse of fair-value accounting is the one that indicts the rules
themselves. All of the others, in our view, represent a disregard for the rules
as they were (and are).

Stock Issued to and Held by SPEs

GAAP and long-established accounting practice do not permit a corporation to record stock as issued unless it has been paid for in cash or its equivalent. Nevertheless, that is what Enron did, to the tune of $1 billion. For
reasons not yet revealed, Andersen either did not discover these accounting
errors or allowed Enron to make them. Correction of the errors in October
2001 contributed to concerns about Enron's accounting. Nor may corporations record income from increases in the value of their own stock. Enron

skirted this prohibition by transferring its stock and contracts with investment banks to purchase its stock to SPEs in exchange for equity in the SPEs. Then, when the market price of Enron stock increased and the SPEs (which accounted for the stock and contracts at fair value) increased their assets, Enron recognized the gains as increases in its equity investments in the SPEs.

Inadequate Disclosure of Related-Party Transactions and Conflicts of Interest

Enron disclosed that it had engaged in transactions with a related party, identified in its proxy statements—but not in its annual 10K report required by the SEC—as Andrew Fastow. The company asserted in footnote 16 of its 10K filed for 2000 that "the terms of the transactions with the Related Party were reasonable compared to those which could have been negotiated with unrelated third parties." This seems implausible on its face; it seems highly unlikely that unrelated third parties would have been offered the same terms as Fastow. Indeed, the Powers Report concludes that Fastow obtained more than $30 million personally from his management of the SPEs that did business with Enron, and that other employees who reported to Fastow received at least another $11 million. Furthermore, a detailed analysis of the Fastow-related SPEs indicates that the outside investors that Fastow solicited for those SPEs obtained multiple millions from investments on which they took little risk and that provided Enron with few benefits, other than providing a vehicle to misreport income and delay reporting losses. These practices appear to have violated both FASB disclosure requirements and the SEC requirement to disclose transactions exceeding $60,000 in which an executive officer of a corporation has a material interest.[15]

Summary

Thus, except for fair-value accounting, GAAP presently covers substantially all of Enron's accounting misstatements. Enron simply failed to follow the existing rules. Furthermore, it appears that Arthur Andersen violated the basic prescriptions of GAAS in conducting an audit that would allow it to state that its audit had complied with generally accepted accounting principles.

Is Enron Alone?

Although it has been the most extensively publicized, the Enron affair unfortunately is not an isolated instance. As we summarized in chapter 1, over the past several years, public attention has focused on a variety of accounting abuses. What kinds of abuses have occurred, and are they now really any more extensive than in years past?

In their highly illuminating book *The Financial Numbers Game,* Charles Mulford and Eugene Comiskey describe many creative and fraudulent accounting practices employed since the late 1990s, based on their examination of reports by the SEC, the press, and corporate financial filings. Readers interested in the details should refer to this excellent work.[16] What we find significant, however, is that the practices Mulford and Comiskey describe do not provide a sweeping indictment either of GAAP or GAAS. The problem again is that the current rules were not followed—or enforced.

Many of the misleading accounting practices they identify are frauds, often involving misstatements of revenue. How can revenues be misstated? Mulford and Comiskey find and count the ways: by booking sales in a period, although the orders were not shipped or shipped later; by recognizing revenue on aggressively sold merchandise that probably will be returned ("channel stuffing"); by recording revenue in the year received, although the services were provided over several years; by booking revenue immediately, although the goods were sold subject to extended payment periods where collection was unlikely; by booking revenue from shipments to a reseller that was not financially viable; by booking sales subject to side agreements that effectively rendered sales agreements unenforceable; and by keeping the books open after the end of an accounting period to record revenue on shipments actually made after the close of the period.[17]

Mulford and Comiskey also document the misrecording of expenses. Some episodes involved booking promotion and marketing expenses to a related, but not consolidated, enterprise, and recognizing revenue on shipments, but not the cost and liability of an associated obligation to repay purchasers for promotion expenses. Several corporations took "big-bath" write-offs when a new chief executive officer took over, a practice that incorrectly reduces future-period expenses. Warranty and bad-debt expenses applicable to a current period were understated. Aggressive capitalization and extended amortization policies were used to reduce current-period expenses. The most egregious example of capitalizing current-period expenses, by WorldCom, occurred in 2002, after the Mulford and Comiskey book was published.

These have not been the only abuses. Corporations have overstated assets by recording receivables to which they had established no legal right (such as claims on common carriers for damaged goods that were not actually submitted, and claims that could probably not be collected). Inventories have been overstated by overcounting and by delaying write-downs of damaged, defective, overstocked, and obsolete goods. Recognitions of declines in the fair-market values of debt and equity securities have been delayed, even though the chances of recovery were remote. Liabilities have been understated, not only for estimated expenses (such as warranties), but also for accounts payable, taxes payable, environmental clean-up costs, and pension and other employee benefits.

In short, the number and variety of accounting abuses is significant. What kinds of firms—and their auditors—have been engaged in these practices, small ones or big ones? The information summarized in chapter 1 and media reports from the past few years clearly suggest that accounting abuses have been uncovered in large, indeed very large, firms. But this development appears to be relatively recent. Systematic study of the available evidence for earlier years indicates that abuses have been concentrated among smaller firms and their external auditors.

The evidence is provided in a study by Beasley, Carcello, and Hermanson, which examined all of the SEC's accounting and auditing enforcement releases (AAERs) issued between 1987 and 1997 that charged registrants with financial fraud.[18] This ten-year period predates the years covered in table 1-1, which summarizes the more notorious accounting abuses by large firms. But the study finds that during the 1987–97 period, accounting problems clearly were concentrated among *smaller* firms: of 204 randomly selected companies of the nearly 300 alleged to have engaged in financial fraud, 78 percent had assets below $100 million. Interestingly, most of these involved senior officers (72 percent of the AAERs named the CEO, 43 percent the CFO) and had weak boards of directors (according to the study's authors). Half the instances of abuse identified by the authors involved improper revenue recognition resulting largely from recording fictitious revenue and premature revenue recognition.[19]

A minority of the corporations and their senior officers paid fines and made monetary settlements to plaintiffs (35 corporations and 30 senior officers). The officers of some 76 corporations lost their jobs and, in the case of 54 corporations, were barred from working for another SEC registrant for a period of time. Only 31 officers were criminally prosecuted, of which 27 were jailed.

To what extent did external auditors fail to do their jobs, and what kinds of firms were they? The study reports that the SEC explicitly named external auditors in 56 of 195 cases (29 percent). Only 10 were from the major accounting firms. The auditor was charged with performing a substandard audit in 26 of the 56 cases (the balance involved insider trading); 9 of the 26 involved major accounting firms.

What did the SEC do about the external auditors who either permitted or abetted material violations of GAAP or who conducted such poor audits that they did not discover what their clients had done? The study by Beasley and his colleagues *does not report any SEC actions against the individual auditors or their firms* who attested that the statements charged by the SEC to be fraudulent conformed to GAAP. We return to this significant finding shortly.

Meanwhile, what about the widely reported trend in "earnings restatements"? How significant are the numbers, and what lies behind them? A study by the Financial Executives International (FEI) sheds light on these questions.[20] The FEI study searched several databases for all mentions of "restatements" due to irregularities or errors, whether reported voluntarily, forced by company auditors, or enforced by the SEC, between 1977 and 2000. The study found a total of 224 restatements between 1977 and 1989 (17 a year on average), 392 during 1990–97 (49 a year), and 464 during 1998–2000 (155 a year).

The same study also documents the most important, nonoverlapping reasons for restatement: revenue misstatement (38 percent), cost understatement (28 percent), understatement of loan losses (9 percent), and issues relating to in-process research and development, or IPR&D (6 percent). Because of the way the FEI gathered its data, small corporations are likely to be underincluded. Nevertheless, of the firms reviewed for which market values were found, 88 percent in the 1977–94 period and 74 percent in the 1995–2000 period had market values before the restatements of less than $500 million.[21] Only 8 percent in the 1977–94 period and 17 percent in the 1995–2000 period had market values of $1 billion or more. The three-day losses in market values due to reductions in share prices when restatements were announced were relatively small before 1998—an average of $0.9 billion a year. But these annual losses were $17 billion in 1998, $24 billion in 1999, and $31 billion in 2000, with the top ten firms making restatements the sources of most of the losses. In total, the losses for all the corporations making restatements were less than 0.2 percent of their total market value.

Palmrose and Scholz have conducted perhaps the most extensive study of earnings restatements to date.[22] These researchers conducted keyword searches of several databases to identify restatements of previously issued financial statements for 1995 through 1999. They identified 492 companies that announced restatements. The number increased each year, as follows: 44, 48, 90, 106, and 204. Most of these were smaller companies (the mean of total assets was $1.1 billion, but the median was $89 million). The most pervasive reason given for the restatements was revenue misstatement (37 percent), although in more than one-third of the restatements, several causes were given. Among them were merger-related items (29 percent) and adjustments of IPR&D write-offs (19 percent). Litigation (primarily securities class actions) was taken against 38 percent of the companies, their officers, and directors. Auditors were included in 35 percent of the actions. Only misstatements of revenue were a significant factor in this litigation.

In sum, the several studies of financial statement restatements yield similar findings. The number of restatements has increased but is still quite small in relation to the 17,000 companies that report to the SEC. Until recently, restatements were more common among smaller companies. The most pervasive reason for restatement is misstatement of revenue. A substantial minority of companies that restate financial statements and a smaller number of their auditors are sued. Investors' losses that possibly result from misstatements that are corrected are small overall, although for individual companies they can be substantial (particularly recently).

These losses, though, understate the total social cost associated with inadequate audits and gross violations of GAAP, because these are not simply a private matter. The Enron debacle and the misstated financial reports of other corporations have imposed substantial costs on other external auditors, who bear higher liability costs and loss of reputation. Investors have also suffered, not just those who held shares in the affected companies, but investors as a class, because valuations across the board appear to have been adversely affected by the crisis in confidence in earnings reports and other financial information.[23]

Why have the numbers of restatements seemingly skyrocketed in the past several years? Three factors appear to be at work. One is that the SEC stepped up its enforcement directed against aggressive accounting, arising out of the concern expressed by former SEC chairman Arthur Levitt about accounting manipulations and IPR&D accounting.[24] The FEI study identifies two other factors. One is that the SEC directed registrants to account for adjustments to prior-period statements, such as errors that previously were considered immaterial, with restatements rather than prospective corrections. Another factor is companies' conceding rather than disputing small restatements to obtain clearance of their registration statements by SEC staff. Accordingly, the substantial increase in the number of restatements in recent years appears to be attributable, at least from the body of evidence we have reviewed, more to a change in the practices of the SEC than to an apparent worsening of corporate accounting practices.

Nonetheless, it is also significant that the number of very large public companies at the center of major accounting controversies has been rising since the late 1990s. What lies behind this trend? The most plausible explanation, although not yet supported by hard proof, lies in the more extensive use of performance-based compensation—earnings-based bonuses and stock options linked to company stock prices.[25] In principle, and perhaps for many companies, performance-based pay should motivate constructive and healthy financial results from companies. This does not appear to have happened with some executives of very large companies, however, for whom the prospect of realizing large short-term bonuses or gains from the exercise of stock options appears to have encouraged the use of aggressive accounting techniques to support earnings and hence stock prices. [26] Admittedly, such strategies may be shortsighted, because eventually the market finds out that revenue and earnings have been distorted. But for managers who can cash in by selling their shares before the stock price drops or who believe they soon really will increase their firms' revenues and net profit growth, the incentives to fudge the numbers may simply be too strong.[27]

Performance-Based Pay and Stock Options

If this analysis proves correct—and whether it is requires more empirical research—the solution is not to ban or restrict performance-based pay, but to design it so that it both rewards managers for increases in the price of their corporations' shares and penalizes them for stock price declines. For this purpose, awards of actual or phantom stock (hypothetical stock used to calculate bonuses or penalties) are superior to stock options. Options are not ideal because they reward managers if the price of shares generally increases and punish them only if the price of their corporations' shares decreases to the extent that their options lose their value. Even then, compliant boards of directors often lower the strike price at which the options can be exercised.

The current situation might be alleviated by providing for more oversight of compensation packages by outside directors and compensation committees that include only outside directors (as new listing requirements of the exchanges now require). More meaningful disclosure in financial statements of the cost to shareholders of employee options would also be helpful, as would effective audits by outside auditors to uncover misleading and fraudulent accounting practices.

We want to underscore here the special importance of more meaningful disclosure of stock options. Currently, they are disclosed in footnote form, but they are not deducted as expenses when granted.[28] Although some observers have argued that footnote disclosure is sufficient to inform investors who really want this information, we see no reason why this form of compensation should be treated differently from deferred pay and company-provided pensions and excluded as an operating expense. Not recognizing the cost of options clearly violates the basic matching concept of accounting, which posits that expenses that generate revenue in a period must be charged against revenue in the same period.

There can be no serious quarrel that stock options have value; all options do. The only question is whether options can be valued in a way that is verifiable. On this issue, supporters of stock option expensing have the upper hand, in our view, thanks to the development of, among other things, the "Black-Scholes" formula for stock option valuation.[29] The authors of this formula demonstrated that the value of stock options depends on the past variation in the price of the underlying stock, the length of the option term, and the interest rate. Each of these variables is readily determined and can be verified, although the formula is based on a number of assumptions.[30]

Opponents of stock option expensing argue that the Black-Sholes valuation method can misstate the true value of options because the options that companies grant their executives typically contain restrictions that are not found in traded options and have maturities that typically are longer than the options that are found in the marketplace. These restrictions, though, can be factored into the Black-Scholes framework and other pricing sources and quantified. The model-estimation procedure, which essentially is similar with respect to uncertainty in the collection of accounts receivable or estimates of the present value of employee benefits, is better than marking the options down all the way to zero—which is the result that opponents of expensing essentially support. Of course, if similar options *are* traded on the stock market, the values of this form of compensation can be determined both readily and accurately. Indeed, the market price of options granted to employees is the opportunity cost of this form of compensation, because it measures the amount the corporation gives up by not selling the options to investors.

The technical objections to the Black-Sholes formula, in any event, do not apply to other methods of valuing options. For example, independent brokers who regularly price options can value them. Corporations also could sell similar options to investors, which would provide a market price for the options granted to employees. Alternatively, corporations could grant stockholders similar options together with dividends or grant stockholders the opportunity to purchase the options under the same terms as those granted to employees.

We do not take seriously the claim, advanced by some opponents of expensing stock options, that doing so would somehow undermine the entrepreneurial drive of new companies, which have used stock options as a compensation device. Admittedly, showing options as an expense would lower reported earnings—by as much as 25 percent among the Standard & Poor's 500 companies in 2001.[31] But cash compensation or compensation in the form of pension and health benefits also lowers earnings, and there is no quarrel with showing these as expense. If new companies deliberately have to mislead investors about their financial condition in order to raise capital, then they should not receive it in the first place.

As fallout of the accounting scandals, cracks began to appear in mid-summer of 2002 in the American business community's previous strong opposition to the expensing of stock options. Until that time, only two major public companies—Boeing and Winn-Dixie—had been reporting the cost to shareholders of stock options as an expense in the income statement. However, by summer of 2002, several other prominent companies—including Bank One, Citigroup, Coca Cola, General Electric, General Motors, Home Depot, and the Washington Post Company—had joined the club, prompting Federal Reserve Board chairman Alan Greenspan to opine that many other companies would follow suit, making it unnecessary for Congress to act.

In our view, it would be inappropriate in any event for Congress to dictate that stock options should be expensed, just as it was inappropriate for Congress to dictate the opposite result in the 1990s. Accounting standard setting, at least in principle, should be free of political influence.[32] That it isn't is a flaw in the current system in the United States, and one that we address shortly in this and the next chapter. Now that some U.S. companies have decided on their own to expense their stock options, the FASB has the necessary "cover" to require the same treatment for all public companies as part of U.S. GAAP (although it need not specify the precise way in which the stock options must be valued). Another reason for the FASB to move on this issue is to keep pace with international standard setters, who, in the summer of 2002, affirmed a proposal to require options to be expensed. It is an encouraging sign that the FASB took this message to heart in August 2002, when the board directed its staff to begin exploring the issue, and later in November, when the board sought comment on the IASB's proposal.

The Problem with Fair Value

Earlier we identified Enron's misuse of fair-value accounting as the one major area where accounting standards, and not just enforcement, have been appropriately called into question. Given the importance of this issue, we elaborate on it further here.

Fair value is the amount for which an asset could be exchanged, or a liability settled, between informed, willing parties on an arm's-length basis. Fair values would not provide a valid measure of the value of an entire company, which is the value of its net assets in use, or present value. But if fair values could be measured reliably, they would be an improvement over many of the numbers currently provided in balance sheets.

This is because many balance sheet numbers do not reflect current values well and often are subject to substantial errors of measurement. For example, fixed assets, such as buildings and equipment, are stated at their original (historical) costs less depreciation. These numbers are not adjusted for changes in price levels. They do not measure the cost of replacing the assets, the value of the fixed assets to the company, or the amounts that could be obtained if these assets were sold. Company-developed intangible assets are written off as if they had no value. A company's liability for fixed-rate bonds is not adjusted to reflect the effect of changes in interest rates. Uncertain estimates must be made of the present value of future pension and employee benefit obligations.

The SEC, the FASB, and the IASB have been attempting to make balance sheets a bit more current by introducing fair values for financial instruments in some circumstances. For example, derivatives not used for hedging (as defined by the FASB) and energy contracts must be marked to market, with gains and losses reported in the income statement, as are debt and equity securities that are regularly traded on recognized exchanges. Similar securities designated as "available for sale" also must be marked to market, but changes in their values are included only in a (supplementary) comprehensive income statement, while exchange-traded debt securities that are held to maturity are not revalued. However, assets transferred to special purpose entities and financial assets held by investment, business development, and venture capital companies must be marked to fair values, whether or not market quotations are available for this purpose. These exceptions, we fear, allow opportunistic managers to manipulate reported net income to the detriment of financial statement users.

The FASB says fair values are to be measured as follows:

> If a quoted market price is not available, the estimate of fair value should be based on the best information available in the circum-stances. The estimate of fair value should consider prices for similar assets or similar liabilities and the results of valuation techniques to the extent available in the circumstances. Examples of valuation tech-niques include the present value of estimated expected future cash flows using discount rates commensurate with the risks involved, option-pricing models, matrix pricing, option-adjusted spread mod-els, and fundamental analysis.[33]

For investment companies, the AICPA states: "In the absence of a quoted market price, amounts representing estimates of fair values using methods applied consistently and determined in good faith by the board of directors should be used."[34]

Many managers and directors may diligently apply careful analysis, objectively determined numbers, reliable models, and good faith to esti-mate these fair values. But some will take advantage of the inherent diffi-culties in making these estimates to produce values that allow them to inflate reported net income.

The major problem is that the variables required to calculate fair values, such as future cash flows and discount rates, are very difficult to estimate and are subject to substantial error. As a result, the values calculated often are not trustworthy. The same set of numbers put into reasonably con-structed yet different models can yield very different results. The estima-tion process is complicated by the fact that estimates are likely to change over time, as market conditions, general and specific prices, and other enterprise operations change. Although managers make formal or informal

estimates of the present values of assets before their purchase, these estimates need only indicate that the present value of net cash flows exceeds
the cost of the asset. Furthermore, this analysis (called "capital budgeting")
is costly.

Not only are fair-value numbers likely to be unreliable, but they may be
deliberately misleading. Managers who want to look as if they had done
well in a particular accounting period can readily increase their estimates of
cash inflows or decrease their estimates of cash outflows that will be generated by an asset, or decrease the applicable discount rate. If their cash flow
estimates turn out to be incorrect (as they inevitably will, even where managers seek only to make unbiased estimates), the managers can argue that
conditions have changed (as they inevitably do). Managers can argue further that they could not reasonably have predicted the changes or that they
did correctly predict a range of outcomes with associated probabilities, and
that the outcome was within that range. External auditors who attest to the
validity of such statements are in danger of devaluing their own reputations
if subsequent events show that the values were substantially misstated.
Indeed, this lack of trustworthiness led the German legislature to prohibit
fair-value measurement as early as the nineteenth century after many
instances of fraud and speculation. For similar reasons, the SEC in its early
years disallowed estimates and appraisals. Our summary of what went
wrong in Enron provides more recent support for this concern.

Lack of trustworthiness is an important reason that fixed and intangible
assets are not periodically restated to fair values. But, as proponents of fair
value for financial assets might argue, while fair values are not allowed for
fixed and intangible assets, they are and can be reliably limited to financial
assets, the fair values of which are closer to value in use and often can be
readily determined. What proponents of fair value may overlook, however,
is an exception provided by the FASB, through which opportunistic managers can subjectively revalue almost any of their assets and carry the
changes in value through to their income statements.

Here is how the exception can work. First, a company can develop a new
product, facility, or business in a wholly owned subsidiary or transfer the
assets the managers want to revalue into a subsidiary. For illustrative purposes, call the subsidiary FV Inc. The corporation now owns FV Inc.'s
stock, which is a financial asset. Large corporations can do this many times

and have a series of subsidiaries—FV1 Inc., FV2 Inc., and so forth. The managers can then exchange the stock in the FVs for stock in another subsidiary that is designated a securities broker-dealer or an investment company (such as a venture capital or business development company). Although FASB accounting standards allow fair valuation of securities only when they have quoted securities-market prices, it makes an exception for these companies, which are required to value all of their investments at fair values.[35] Because the FV Inc. shares are not traded, their values necessarily must come from the corporate managers' estimates of the fair values of the underlying assets, including intangibles. Finally, because the subsidiaries are wholly owned by the corporation, they must be consolidated with the parent, which now puts the revalued assets on the corporation's consolidated financial statements. The net result: almost any group of assets can be revalued to what the managers say they are worth, and changes in those valuations (usually increases, we expect) are reported as part of income.[36]

To be sure, fair values based on unreliable market data are not the only nonmarket estimates used in accounting. Allowances for doubtful accounts and for returned goods and warranties, periodic depreciation and amortization, liability for pensions and other future employee benefits, and the cost of employee stock options are some of the more important items that must be estimated. It bears emphasis, however, that these estimates are made to report liabilities and expenses that apply to revenue recognized in a particular period. They are usually made using prestructured procedures that limit managerial manipulation. Furthermore, the alternative is not to report the liabilities and expenses. In contrast, the fair values about which we are concerned relate primarily to assets, which we fear can be (and in some cases already have been) used by managers to inflate reported income.[37]

In making our criticism of fair-value accounting, we do not want to be misconstrued as arguing that *no* fair values can be or should be presented to investors and or even attested to by outside auditors. We are simply arguing that for purposes of determining *reported net income*, fair values should not be used for assets that are not traded in "thick" public markets. We fully support the use of fair values—by which we mean *market* values—for assets that *are* traded in markets that generate reliable pricing information. Meanwhile, investors and others who want to know the market value of the enterprise must and can look to other sources of information.

The Failure in Enforcement

So far, we have argued that the main disclosure problems lie not in the rules, but in the failure to ensure compliance with them. These enforcement failures, moreover, appear to be systemic. By that we mean that each of the various institutions, mechanisms, or gatekeepers set up to ensure proper disclosure—corporate managers and directors, auditors, public and private regulators, even the threat of criminal sanctions (for fraud) or civil liability (for negligence)—has failed to some degree.

We concentrate here on the failure of auditors—as well as failures to properly regulate and oversee auditors—because they are supposed to form the first line of defense against improper accounting. But before we do, we briefly address one concern: that the proliferation of accounting problems stems from a "weakening" of the federal securities laws governing auditor liability—the Private Securities Litigation Reform Act of 1995 (PSLRA), which generally made it more difficult for class action plaintiffs to sue public firms for accounting abuses; and the Securities Litigation Uniform Standards Act of 1998 (SLASA), which abolished state court class actions alleging securities fraud. Specifically, is it true that these laws have made it so difficult to sue accounting firms that auditors have since relaxed their guard on the firms they are supposed to watch? Columbia Law School professor John Coffee points to this legislation and two court cases that made bringing lawsuits against auditors more costly to plaintiffs as possible explanations for the presumed weakening of auditing performance.[38] Although he supports the changes on grounds of fairness, he concludes that "their collective impact was to appreciably reduce the risk of liability."[39]

We are not convinced, however, that the recent legislation can be blamed for the recent rise in earnings restatements and accounting abuses more generally. For one thing, as we have noted, there is evidence that some portion of the increase in the number of earnings restatements may be more attributable to changes in SEC practices than to an increase in the underlying tendency of corporations to misstate their financial positions and of their auditors to go along with those decisions. More significantly, however, the PSLRA did not exempt auditors from liability; it simply cut back their joint and several liability for accounting misdeeds when several defendants are before the court.[40] The PSLRA also raised pleading standards and no longer allowed plaintiffs to seek treble damages. The rationales for these reforms were to prevent plaintiffs from digging into the deepest pockets among a group of defendants, regardless of the degree of culpability of individual defendants, and from bringing extortionate lawsuits against external auditors in the hope of a settlement. Meanwhile, the SLASA only abolished state court class actions alleging securities fraud; federal class actions can still be brought against accountants.

That the recent legislation has not significantly reduced the threat of liability for financial malfeasance is reflected in the litigation data. In particular, in the five years before the PLSRA was enacted, shareholders filed 948 suits; in the five years since, the number is virtually unchanged, at 935.[41]

Moreover, we are not aware that any accounting firm named as a defendant in any of the large recent accounting controversies, such as those listed in table 1-1, has been excused from liability or not been added as a defendant in any of these actions because of the recent federal securities legislation. To underline the point, plaintiffs clearly have not been dissuaded from suing Arthur Andersen for liability in Enron and other cases.

We return, therefore, to the central question at issue: had external auditors been more diligent in examining and evaluating their clients' records and financial statements, as required by GAAS, many, perhaps most, of the recent earnings misstatements could have been caught and stopped. We caution, though, that the cost of avoiding all audit and reporting shortcomings probably is excessive. The fraud and restatement studies by Beasley and his colleagues, the FEI, and Palmrose and Scholz, all find relatively few instances of financial statement problems among the 17,000 SEC registrants. Hence, investors could be worse off (because their companies would have added expenses) if much more extensive auditing requirements were imposed on all corporations.

Auditors are not the only ones at fault. Several bodies that oversee both individual auditors and the firms they work for, all seem to have failed in their duties as well. The AICPA, for example, the self-regulatory body for the auditing profession, has a committee that is supposed to discipline wayward auditors. According to a study conducted by the *Washington Post,* which examined more than ten years of SEC professional misconduct cases against accountants, "the AICPA took disciplinary action against fewer than 20 percent of those accountants already sanctioned by the Commission.

Moreover, even when the AICPA found that the accountants so sanctioned had committed violations, the Association closed the vast majority of ethics cases without taking disciplinary action or publicly disclosing the results, but instead issued confidential letters simply directing the offenders to undergo training." [42] Clearly, "self-regulation" by the AICPA has not been very effective, nor can it be expected to be: the most stringent penalty the AICPA can apply is to expel the offending member from the organization. [43]

What about state regulators? The record here is not much better. By and large, state offices that regulate professionals such as accountants are not well funded or staffed with enough trained individuals to both ferret out and investigate accounting misconduct, especially the kinds of complex accounting machinations revealed in some of the large company scandals of recent years. In general, state regulators tend to act after a client or other government agency has successfully brought a legal action against an accountant or when an offending accountant cannot respond adequately to a serious complaint. Indeed, the *Washington Post* study found that "the state of New York, which had the most accountants sanctioned by the SEC, as of June 2002 had disciplined [only] 17 of 49 New York accountants." [44]

And, finally, what about the SEC? To its credit, the SEC has been more aggressive in recent years investigating companies' financial statements to determine whether earnings have been misrepresented. As we have already suggested, this effort started under former SEC chairman Arthur Levitt, and was continued under its next chairman, Harvey L. Pitt.

SEC action is important because it can trigger several consequences: private lawsuits against company officers and directors for negligence or even willful commission of fraud or misrepresentation; similar lawsuits against accounting firms; and, if the facts warrant, even criminal fraud investigations by the Department of Justice. Because these consequences have been apparent for some time, the puzzle is why they have not done more to deter the kind of accounting abuses that seem to have become more frequent in recent years. One reason may be that the SEC has rarely disciplined accountants and auditing firms who inappropriately attested to financial statements. Another possibility is that what, in principle, should deter *entire firms* from misconduct may not work for *individual external auditors*, particularly those whose salaries and bonuses depend on how much business they bring in (or work on) and whose liability costs may be covered by insurance or the firm (or both).

Indeed, an individual partner of a large accounting firm who is in charge of a single very large client has considerable incentives to accede to the demands of that client. If the partner does not and loses the account for the firm, the partner may lose a substantial amount of personal income, if not his or her position in the firm. If a partner does accede to the demands of the company, however, three things might happen, none of which may be unduly onerous to that individual. First, the misstatements might not be discovered. Second, if the errors are discovered, the partner-in-charge might not be blamed. Third, if blamed, the other partners are likely to defend the errant partner to avoid having to assume substantial damages, since legally they are jointly responsible for their partner's misconduct.

Considering the externalities that accompany major audit failures, there must be some institutional mechanism that can discipline individual external auditors who fail to live up to their professional responsibilities. If neither the AICPA nor the states can do this job, the responsibility should lie with the SEC. In this respect, we do find fault with the commission. Although the SEC has the authority under Rule 201.102 (e) to discipline accountants who attest to financial statements that violate GAAP or GAAS, it has used that power sparingly. We can understand why the commission has not used its ultimate weapon—prohibiting an offending *firm* from attesting to financial statements of public companies—except in cases of gross malfeasance or criminal conduct, as was the case with Arthur Andersen. But we have a harder time understanding why the commission has so rarely sanctioned *individual auditors* who have attached their firm's names to the financial statements that included the substantial violations outlined above. If individual CPAs had reason to believe that their professional careers and personal wealth were seriously in jeopardy, they would be much more likely to risk losing a client rather than to agree to that client's demands for inadequate audits and overly aggressive or significantly misleading accounting. This personal concern would be enhanced, we suggest, if the partner-in-charge and confirming partner were required to sign their own names, as well as their firm's name, to attestations.

We are hopeful that this failure to sanction errant accountants will change now that Congress has established the new Public Company

Accounting Oversight Board.[45] The board is to have five "financially liter-
ate" full-time members, only two of whom shall be or have been certified
public accountants. The board will register public accounting firms, establish standards related to the preparation of audit reports, conduct inspec-
tions of accounting firms, and conduct investigations and disciplinary proceedings. It then may impose appropriate sanctions, presumably against
both firms and individual accountants.

Beyond Enron:
Problems with Setting U.S. Accounting Standards

Regardless of what one may think about specific accounting rules, there are
reasons to be concerned about the *process* by which accounting standards
are set, at least in the United States. By outlining these concerns, which
have been voiced by others, we do not mean to demean the professionalism of those who are members of the FASB or who serve on its staff. These
are dedicated individuals, with great expertise, operating under very difficult, often highly politically charged, circumstances.

The problems we outline instead flow from the circumstance in which
the FASB has been placed: as the sole, or monopoly, standard setter for
accounting. As we have discussed, there are virtues in having a single set of
standards—investors can more readily understand the meaning and limitations of the numbers presented in financial statements, and they can
more effectively compare the financial performance of different firms. But
these virtues can be overstated. Even though U.S. GAAP is highly detailed,
it still leaves room in plenty of areas for firms and their accountants to
exercise their judgment, such as how and when to provide for uncol-
lectibles, the length of time over which to depreciate fixed assets and the
method for doing so, and how to account for inventories. Furthermore,
corporate managers determine the groupings of data that are relevant to
their firms, such as choice of product lines and definitions of operating
profit. When different firms, even those operating under the same set of
standards, exercise their judgment on these matters in different ways, the
results can be something less than the apples-to-apples comparisons that
advocates of a single body of accounting standards sometimes claim.

In any event, any benefits gained from having a single standard setter must be balanced against the costs. And there are at least three major criticisms of the way the FASB, like any monopoly, has operated. One problem is that it has no incentive to act quickly. The FASB has considered the issue of expensing stock options since the early 1990s and by the end of 2002 still had not resolved the matter. Similarly, the FASB debated accounting standards for derivatives for several years before finally acting. Since 1982, the board has been considering an overall policy on consolidations, including accounting for thinly capitalized SPEs; the SPE portion of the project was dealt with only in 2002.[46] Other examples could be given as well.

Second, the rules under U.S. GAAP are highly detailed, much more so than under the international standard. A prime example is the set of rules on derivatives, which runs on for more than 800 pages. The FASB has been driven to write its rules in a highly detailed fashion because of pressure by certain of its major constituents—publicly held firms and their accountants—to provide more certainty as a way to protect them against liability claims and regulatory sanctions. To his credit, the new chairman of the FASB, Robert Herz, has promised a rewrite of GAAP to make it less detailed and more user friendly.[47] Whether he will be able to pull off such an enormous task remains to be seen.

Third, and perhaps most important, in the past the FASB has been heavily influenced by certain constituent groups. For example, despite its expressed preference for fair value for financial instruments, the FASB (with the concurrence of the SEC) has given in to pressure from banks and permits companies to exclude from their operating income statements revaluation gains and losses on securities (for which reliable market values are readily available) other than those held in trading accounts. Market values of securities that are held to maturity are not even used for the balance sheet. Meanwhile, pressure from the business community—high-tech firms in particular—apparently has kept the FASB from requiring corporations to show as expenses the economic values of compensation in the form of options granted to employees, even though this violates the matching principle (whereby appropriate expenses are matched with the income they generate).[48]

There is a respectable view that politics is inherent in any rulemaking process, especially one that is supposed to be in the public interest, and so we should simply live with the fact. Moreover, it can be reasonably claimed that setting accounting standards is not a science. Any number of accounting issues generate reasonable differences of opinion. No one should pretend, therefore, that accounting standards are a subject so pure that they should not be affected by the views of the profession that applies them or the firms that have to abide by them.

At the same time, however, it is vital to remember that accounting standards that are attested to by external auditors should help investors make projections about future cash flows and evaluate managerial performance. The standards should be based on a coherent and consistent model of what is reported and how it is reported—one that allows users to determine efficiently the meaning and usefulness of the numbers. Where the standards are changed or not implemented out of concern for the managers of the affected firms rather than investors, who tend not to be organized and who rarely can effectively lobby Congress or the FASB on a particular rule, the outcome often is not socially desirable.[49]

In short, it is not that politics should be kept out of the rulemaking process—it probably never can be—but that the current system, at times, can too heavily favor narrow interests over the interests of investors as a class, a problem that is not unique to accounting standards. It would be preferable, as we suggest in the next chapter, to allow investors to factor into their investment decisions the choice corporations make about which set of accounting standards to use. Corporations then would have an incentive to provide investors with information that is useful to them or face an increased cost of capital should investors be dissatisfied.

3 | *Fixing Corporate Disclosure*

Many proposals for "fixing" the U.S. disclosure system have been offered, and as we discuss in this chapter, some have been enacted by Congress and signed into law by the president. But while policymakers deliberated, the market itself engaged in a lot of "self-correction." Managers and directors of many companies began paying far more attention to disclosure, and some companies whose stock prices dropped sharply right after Enron's failure—among them, AIG, GE, and IBM—provided more details about their operations and risks. The various private gatekeepers who failed so miserably in Enron—external auditors, analysts, investment banks, and ratings agencies—also tightened up their practices. Both the New York Stock Exchange (NYSE) and the NASDAQ issued far-reaching proposals that would force managers and boards of directors of corporations listed on their exchanges to be more accountable to shareholders.[1] Boards themselves took steps on their own initiative to become more vigilant about accounting and disclosure practices.[2] Institutional investors, including labor unions and pension funds, began demanding changes in investment banking practices (such as

49

not allowing research analysts to profit from investment banking business) and auditing relationships (such as prohibiting external auditors from engaging in nonaudit and tax business for the companies they audited). The SEC also became more aggressive about pursuing accounting misstatements since Enron's problems surfaced. And insurers who provide liability coverage for directors and officers of corporations have begun to demand far more information from those companies before they extend insurance or price it.

Has "the problem" been fixed? To some extent, the answer to that question is yes. But certain of the so-called solutions are likely, in our view, to be ineffectual or even counterproductive. Other fixes have been implemented, but it is too soon to judge their effectiveness. In this chapter, we attempt to sort out the various reforms, both those that have already been implemented and those we believe should be adopted. We divide our discussion of remedies into three areas: accounting standards specifically related to Enron; the process of setting accounting standards generally; and upgrading the enforcement of accounting and auditing standards, whether through better oversight or better incentives.

Specific Accounting Standards Related to the Enron Scandal

We begin with the controversy surrounding the failure of Enron that has so far attracted the most public attention: the creation of multiple highly leveraged special purpose entities that the company used to finance a series of ventures, many of which lost money. As we discussed in chapter 2, under prevailing Generally Accepted Accounting Principles, sponsors of SPEs such as Enron were required to consolidate the assets and liabilities of these entities with those of the sponsor only if outside investors contributed less than 3 percent of the SPE's assets (assuming the sponsoring corporation did not own a majority of its voting stock or, in fact, control the SPE or garner its risks and rewards). In uncharacteristically rapid fashion, the FASB responded to the furor raised over the 3 percent rule by proposing in May 2002 that the minimum investment by outside investors be increased to 10 percent of total assets. This may be a wise proposal, but the Enron case does not justify it one way or the other.

As we noted in the last chapter, Enron apparently misled its auditor, Arthur Anderson, with respect to the adequacy of the 3 percent rule in a number of Enron-sponsored SPEs, and to this extent Enron inappropriately failed to consolidate those investments on its balance sheet and income statement. This looks like old-fashioned fraud or gross negligence and should be remedied through civil or criminal litigation, or both. Furthermore, Enron failed to disclose the extent and details of its guarantees of the debt of its many SPEs, as is required under GAAP (FAS 5). It is plausible that if these disclosures had been made, Enron never would have been able to leverage itself to the extent, nor take the risks, that it did.

A more important accounting policy issue revealed by the Enron situation has received much less attention, however. That is the company's misuse of fair-value accounting to overstate the values on certain of its financial assets for which there were no broadly traded markets, thereby covering up losses on other assets and operations. As we described in chapter 2, present GAAP standards allow almost any large company to convert fixed and intangible assets to financial assets and then to overstate their values, with the increases reported as current income. For this reason, we urge that both of the world's leading standard setters—the FASB and the IASB—abandon the efforts to further the use of fair values. Instead, both bodies should simply require that all financial assets held by any company (including investment companies) be valued at their *market values* only where those assets are traded in "thick" markets where the values are trustworthy and verifiable. At the same time, we favor using market values where they are based on relevant transactions that yield trustworthy prices and can be verified with reasonable effort by an auditor.

In the previous chapter we also urged that GAAP be modified to require companies to treat employee stock options as expenses, as are other forms of compensation. Stock options are no different from deferred salary, pensions, or other employee benefits, with two exceptions. One is that options may encourage corporate managers to take actions that enhance option value at the expense of shareholders. Such actions include increasing risk, which makes options more valuable; repurchasing stock, which mechanically increases per-share market price (as fewer shares are outstanding); and hiding debt and manipulating and falsifying reported net income, which may increase share price, at least temporarily. Not treating the options as an expense inflates reported net income and possibly also inflates share prices. Boards of directors may have granted managers stock options too freely, because they did not appear to cost anything—the "bottom line," after all, was not affected.

The other exception is that the cost to shareholders of employee stock options is difficult to measure. But, then, so are pensions and other future employee benefits. Yet, these forms of compensation are expenses and should be recognized as such. In chapter 2, we outlined several procedures that could be used to measure the present economic cost of stock options. These include option-pricing models, investment bankers' valuations, and issuance of similar options to shareholders. We prefer the last method, because it provides a market price that is trustworthy.

Accounting Standards Generically

Beyond the specific accounting questions that the Enron and other recent accounting controversies may raise is the much broader, and more difficult, issue of whether the process of *setting* accounting standards—specifically U.S. GAAP by the FASB—should be changed or even replaced. We discussed in the last chapter the three main charges that have been leveled against the FASB and its decisionmaking process: it is too slow; it results in rules that are excessively detailed; and it is too vulnerable to narrow private sector interests at the expense of the wider public interest. We now examine three very different broad approaches for remedying these flaws: fixing the FASB standard-setting process with incremental reforms; replacing U.S. GAAP with International Financial Reporting Standards (IFRS); or introducing some form of competition between the two sets of standards.

Incremental Reforms

The least disruptive, but also the least bold, of the approaches for correcting the flaws in the current standard-setting process is to adopt various incremental reforms, while essentially keeping the system intact. For example, to speed up the rulemaking process, the SEC could impose deadlines on rule changes, with the threat that the commission would take action by a certain date if the FASB did not act.[3] The SEC could also become more proactive in reviewing, if not actually setting, the FASB's rulemaking agenda on a regular basis. One drawback to this approach, however, is that it would put the SEC explicitly in charge of rules governing privately held companies that do not have to register with the SEC, since FASB rules apply to all firms, whether or not they must comply with SEC registration requirements.

The FASB itself, meanwhile, seems ready to tackle the second main complaint against its rules—that precisely because these rules are so detailed, they invite loophole chasing by clever accountants, attorneys, and investment bankers, who advise their clients on how to obey the letter but not the spirit of the rules. Such advice generally results in financial statements that do not fairly represent the financial condition of the enterprise according to the principles implicit in GAAP. As we noted in the last chapter, incoming FASB chairman Robert Herz has promised to address this criticism by initiating a major rewrite of U.S. GAAP aimed at making the standards both more transparent and more flexible. If successful, this overhaul would move U.S. GAAP in the direction of IFRS.[4]

The incremental solution for excessive political influence, at least in principle, is for Congress to keep its hands off the rulemaking process—not just directly, but indirectly, by abstaining from placing any pressure on the SEC, which oversees the FASB.[5]

Merely listing these possible reforms should suggest the difficulty of implementing them to bring about real change. Having the SEC as a backstop to the FASB could speed up the rulemaking process, but at the cost of placing even greater political pressure on it. That is because the SEC itself is subject to congressional oversight, and Congress has not been shy about expressing its views on disclosure issues. Furthermore, it is for this reason that it is unlikely that Congress can convincingly address the political influence problem. Even a strong congressional resolution expressing the body's desire to remain neutral on standards questions does not bind the current Congress, let alone future assemblies.

As for the FASB's rule-rewriting project, we sincerely hope that it is successful. But the effort will take time. It is also likely that any rewritten standards would not remain simple for long. After all, a major reason why U.S. GAAP has become so detailed is that accountants and companies have

wanted greater specificity to help reduce exposure to liability that rules
with more discretion, like those of the IFRS, might entail. If U.S. GAAP
were overhauled, this desire for specificity would not disappear; rather, it is
more likely to increase as economic changes give rise to more uncertainties
and as different methods are adopted to deal with these events. Over time,
therefore, any revised rules are likely to revert gradually to the details for
which they are now criticized.

In most instances, incremental solutions to policy problems are adopted
because consensus is harder to develop around more radical alternatives.
Correcting the flaws relating to the current accounting standard-setting
process may be an exception to this pattern. Here, incremental steps either
may not satisfactorily address the shortcomings or may not be forthcoming at all. More fundamental reforms may be both more feasible and more
constructive.

A Single World Standard?

Even before the Enron affair, a growing disjunction was apparent, at least to
knowledgeable observers, between the globalization of the capital markets
and the system of national disclosure regimes. With investors increasingly
moving funds across national borders into shares of firms incorporated or
doing business in different countries, isn't it about time that publicly held
firms in different countries comply with a single set of reporting standards?

In principle, there should be several benefits from having a single set of
standards. Making it easier for investors to compare financial statements of
firms in different countries should reduce the risks investors face and thus
lower the cost of capital. It also should improve the allocation of capital
across national boundaries, by helping investors allocate their funds to their
most profitable uses, adjusted for risk. Indeed, investors themselves seem to
recognize these virtues. In a survey conducted by McKinsey and Company,
reported in the summer of 2002, 90 percent of large institutional investors
worldwide want companies to report their results under a single world
standard, although European and American investors have very different
preferences: 78 percent of Western Europeans favored the international
accounting standards set by the IASB, while 76 percent of the Americans
preferred U.S. GAAP.[6]

Figure 3-1. *Portfolio Equity Outflows as Percent of Gross Domestic Product, 1992–2000*

Percent of GDP

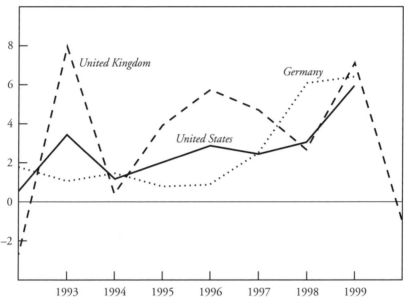

Source: International Financial Statistics CD-ROM, International Monetary Fund, 2001. Outflows are the change in portfolio equity assets during the year.

That markets have become increasingly global in character is evident in figures 3-1 and 3-2, which depict annual outflows and inflows of portfolio equity, or net purchases of securities in either direction, as percentages of gross domestic product during the 1990s for the three countries where most of the world's equity trading takes place: Germany, the United Kingdom, and the United States. For the most part, the figures show an increasing trend toward greater portfolio capital movements, although with significant year-to-year variation. Total cross-border portfolio equity flows among developed markets now exceed $1 trillion annually.[7]

Gross purchases of equities are much greater in volume. Gross annual purchases by foreigners of U.S. equities in the year 2000 totaled $7 trillion. The comparable figure for gross purchases by U.S. residents of foreign

Figure 3-2. *Portfolio Equity Inflows as Percent of Gross Domestic Product, 1992–2000*

Percent of GDP

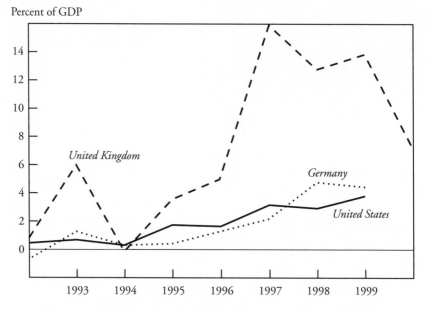

Source: International Financial Statistics CD-ROM, International Monetary Fund, 2001. Inflows are the change in portfolio equity liabilities during the year.

securities was $3.6 trillion. These figures had risen by roughly a factor of ten or more since 1990.[8]

Another indicator of the growing integration of capital markets is the rising number of cross-listings by corporations whose shares are traded on both the New York and London stock exchanges, illustrated in figure 3-3. Because companies that cross-list incur the expense of complying with the rules of multiple exchanges, they must believe that the benefits of reaching a wider base of potential investors and making themselves more attractive to customers and suppliers more than justify the costs. A substitute for cross-listings, at least for trading in U.S. and European markets, is for foreign companies to trade as a depository receipt (DR).[9] Trading in DRs in the United States in 2000 exceeded $1 trillion, or about 17 percent of trading in corresponding local markets. In that same year, 115 DR offerings

Figure 3-3. *International Companies Listed on Major Exchanges as Proportion of Total Listings, 1993–2000*

Percent of GDP

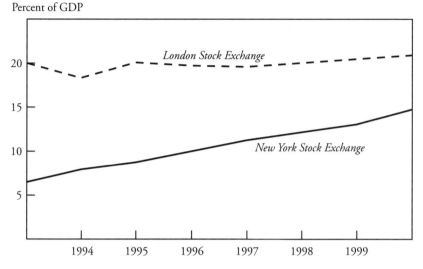

Sources: www.londonstockexchange.com/market/historic.asp; www.nyse.com/pdfs/nonussum 010813.pdf; www.nyse.com/pdfs/10_HISTORICAL.pdf.

took place in the United States and Europe, a 32 percent increase over 1999.[10]

Ironically, the new listing requirements of the New York Stock Exchange discussed later—which apply to foreign and domestic firms alike—may discourage listings of some foreign companies that cannot meet the new rules (especially those relating to the independence of board members), and to this extent, therefore, may slow down the globalization of equities markets, at least in the short run. Furthermore, measures of cross-border integration based solely on volumes of flows can be misleading because equities markets are far from perfectly integrated, even among developed economies where one would expect political and legal risks, as well as information disclosure, to be roughly comparable.[11] Rather, investors tend to have a "home country" bias, in that they typically have far lower proportions of their portfolios invested in foreign stocks than is indicated by the relative valuations of those stocks as a share of the worldwide market.[12]

This preference for home-country markets can be explained by a variety of factors, including language barriers, currency exchange risk, and higher transactions costs on foreign stock purchases, variations in corporate governance, and risk aversion on the part of investors to putting their money into companies with which they are not familiar. Yet the disparity in the kind and quality of information disclosed by companies in different countries undoubtedly plays a contributing role.

By implication, therefore, if publicly held firms around the world all had to play by the same reporting rules—in the way they calculate their financial position and in the way published data are verified and audited—some of the home-country bias very likely would be reduced. This, in essence, is one of the strongest rationales for having a single set of accounting standards apply in all markets, and especially in the world's largest capital market, the United States.

Since the rest of the world is well on its way to adopting IFRS, there are two practical ways of getting to a single set of standards: either the FASB harmonizes U.S. GAAP with IFRS, or the FASB accepts replacement of U.S. GAAP with the international standards. In the wake of the Enron affair, some find appealing the claim that the international standards, in fact, are *superior* to U.S. GAAP. In particular, critics of U.S. GAAP suggest that the IFRS approach of having companies report according to the substance of a situation would have prevented Enron and its auditor, Arthur Andersen, from avoiding consolidation of the SPEs that Enron in effect controlled.[13] More broadly, the fact that the IASB has endorsed stock option expensing, whereas the FASB has not, seems to add another argument in favor of the international standards. The excessive detail of U.S. GAAP relative to the IFRS provides yet another arrow in the quiver of advocates of the international standards. For these and perhaps other reasons, if IFRS were truly superior to U.S. GAAP, replacing U.S. GAAP with IFRS clearly would reduce the risks of investing in companies that convert to IFRS, thus lowering their cost of capital.

How valid are each of these arguments in favor of a single set of accounting standards, and the use of IFRS worldwide in particular? It is appropriate to begin with the globalization of securities markets, which provides the strongest rationale for unified standards. To an important degree, the extent to which markets have become truly globalized is somewhat overstated. National exchanges still very much compete with one another, and indeed, below we suggest that even greater competition may be a good thing.

The belief or perception that a single standard—the IFRS in particular—would facilitate comparisons of financial performance of companies in different countries also is overstated, in our view. The general, principles-based nature of the international rules necessarily means that companies using IFRS already have some significant degree of reporting discretion. The greater is this freedom, the less comparability there must be among financial statements of different companies (although with greater flexibility, firms might report accurately and fairly). Meanwhile, even the more detailed U.S. GAAP rules allow companies flexibility in reporting their financial results. Among other things, they can choose different depreciation schedules for fixed assets, make varying estimates of uncollected accounts, use different assumptions in determining the values of inventories (first-in, first-out or last-in, first-out), and make assumptions necessary to estimate the cost of employee benefits that will be paid in the future. In short, even within the United States, investors should not assume that they can now easily make apples-to-apples comparisons of the financial reports of U.S. companies.

As for the claim that international standards are superior to U.S. GAAP, there may be some merit to it on certain issues, such as expensing of stock options and consolidation of off-balance sheet entities. But the more specific U.S. GAAP rules might be better suited to the litigious U.S. legal system, if they provide corporate officers and external auditors with more certainty and protection from unjustified lawsuits. In any event, as we show in the appendix to this chapter, the differences between IFRS and GAAP are not as significant as they are made out to be.

Whatever the merits of IFRS relative to U.S. GAAP may be, we are skeptical that a move toward the universal adoption of the international standards would satisfactorily address the flaws for which the current standard-setting process in the United States has been criticized. This is because replacing one standard-setting monopoly with another—or keeping both standard-setting bodies in place with virtually identical standards—is not likely to lead to a net improvement. In some respects the result could even be counterproductive.

For example, there is no guarantee that moving the standard setter from Connecticut (headquarters of the FASB) to London (the location of the IASB) will speed up accounting rulemaking. At fourteen members, the IASB board is twice the size of the FASB seven-member board, and its size would increase if the United States came on board. Larger boards can take longer to reach decisions. The fact that the IASB's members often have experience with different national standards setters, each with its own views and institutional history, can further complicate decisionmaking.

What about the alternative approach to achieving a single standard—harmonizing the two major standards, U.S. GAAP and IFRS? This is the approach that both the FASB and the IASB adopted in their joint announcement in September 2002 to eliminate all of the major differences between the two standards by 2005.

In principle, the announced harmonization exercise might make it easier for both the FASB and the IASB to fend off the kind of political pressure to bend rules in a particular fashion that has plagued the FASB in the past. Both bodies presumably can now deflect this pressure by pointing to the need to compromise with the other body. But this outcome is not assured. Business interests simply may step up their lobbying efforts on both sides of the Atlantic to secure outcomes to their liking. Indeed, certain industries that are active globally—such as financial services and automobile manufacturing—may be advantaged under such a system. Moreover, nothing would prevent the business community (or segments of it) from going directly to Congress to persuade it to override any particular standard, whether issued by the FASB, the IASB, or both (just as business interests persuaded Congress to prevent the FASB from issuing a rule in the 1990s that would have required expensing of stock options). The same is true in Europe, where individual countries retain the right to reject individual international standards if they so choose.

More fundamentally, a central problem with either the replacement or harmonization approaches to achieving uniformity in standards is that the resulting single body of standards could easily fragment over time. Under either option, the FASB is likely to continue to exist in order to interpret the international standards for the U.S. context, since users of accounting standards in the United States, including companies and their auditors, are likely to continue demanding the greater certainty that more specific rules can promise. Other nations may keep their accounting bodies for similar reasons. Furthermore, as experience with the IFRS in Europe has shown, companies and their accountants in countries with different languages, legal systems, and customs tend to describe, interpret, and apply apparently similar terms differently. Over time, therefore, these national rulings and interpretations would lead to multiple versions of the IFRS and resurrect the disorder in accounting standards across national boundaries that now has many calling for the international standards to replace U.S. GAAP.

In sum, moving to a single worldwide set of accounting standards is not the panacea for the problems presently said to be plaguing U.S. GAAP. For one thing, a harmonized set of standards is hardly assured. Melding the principles-based approach of the IFRS with the rules-based philosophy embodied in U.S. GAAP is likely to prove very difficult, even with the best of announced intentions of the IASB and the FASB. But even if the two standard setters could surmount their philosophical problem, we believe the inherent limitations of accounting and the range of acceptable but different procedures for recording many important transactions and accruals are likely to prevent investors from making the very comparisons that are the primary rationale for a single set of international standards in the first place.

Competition in Standards

A central problem with any monopoly standard setter—whether it be the FASB, the IASB, or any other similar body—is that it has no incentive to respond quickly to market forces, let alone keep its actions free of political influence. As in private markets, the solution to monopoly is competition. Although there are differences between competition among standard setters and competition among private firms, there is also a key similarity: in both contexts the presence of more than one provider helps to keep all on their toes and more responsive to the interests of users than is the case under monopoly. [14] Although standard setters do not have to satisfy the test of profitability that is the yardstick of success, if not survival, of private firms, the standards they set do have to be sufficiently widely adopted by companies to be taken seriously. If they are not, their executives and staff lose prestige and are increasingly seen as irrelevant. When that happens, they lose funding support. So, even though standard-setting organizations do not sell a product for a price or seek to maximize the wealth of their owners, they have a similar interest in satisfying users of their product (accounting standards). As is the situation for business competition, investors benefit from competition among product providers.

In the disclosure arena, competition can come in various forms. The most ambitious approach, one we call *controlled competition*, would let publicly listed corporations in the United States choose whether to use U.S. GAAP or IFRS as their reporting standard, provided that once they made a choice, they could not change standards for some set period. A key element of this option is that corporations would not be required to reconcile their financial statements to the standard not chosen, as foreign firms listing on U.S. exchanges and choosing international standards are now required to do.

We label this option controlled competition because, as a practical matter, it envisions only two competing standards: IFRS and U.S. GAAP. European firms, however, would not be able to choose U.S. GAAP, because the European Commission (EC) has adopted a regulation requiring them to report only under IFRS by 2005. However, if the United States allowed European corporations listed in the United States to use IFRS only, it is conceivable that the EC would allow European corporations to report under U.S. GAAP only, if they so chose.

An alternative, somewhat less ambitious, approach would allow more competition among *exchanges* by permitting investors in participating countries to access foreign stocks directly within their home-country borders (for example, through computer screens based there) rather than having to engage a foreign broker to execute trades abroad. A new Council on Foreign Relations study recommends this option, not just for reporting standards, but also for the entire system of disclosure and corporate governance rules.[15] In particular, the study suggests a system of *mutual recognition,* wherein host countries, such as the United States, would allow exchanges from other countries with acceptable disclosure regimes to impose their own rules on corporations whose shares are initially listed on those exchanges, but that are also traded on exchanges in the host country, provided those countries afford U.S. exchanges reciprocal rights. In this way, competition among exchanges, each with different listing requirements, would bring about competition in disclosure systems, including accounting standards.[16]

The exchange-competition model, however, has two substantive drawbacks relative to the firm-choice model. For one thing, embracing exchange competition requires a tolerance for competition among *entire systems* of corporate governance, insofar as these systems are the subject of listing requirements of the exchanges. In contrast, a policy of allowing firms on any exchange to choose their own reporting standard (within a predefined list) entails a much more limited form of competition. Second, for firms to choose among reporting standards under the exchange-competition model, the firms must actually list their shares on another exchange. Listing on multiple exchanges may not be as burdensome as it once was—after all, as we have noted, the number of firms whose shares are cross-listed has been rising over time. Still, multiple listing entails some additional cost. In contrast, if firms listed on a single exchange are allowed to choose among reporting standards, they need not pay the additional expense associated with listing on another exchange simply to take advantage of its different disclosure system.[17]

Whether implemented by allowing firms to choose their standard or by allowing mutual recognition of exchanges, controlled competition at least offers the opportunity of addressing the main weaknesses of a monopoly-based standard-setting system. Competition, even in the controlled fashion we have outlined, should stimulate competing standard setters to keep pace with market developments and thus help cure the foot-dragging problem that has dogged the FASB (and that very likely would plague the IASB if it were given a worldwide monopoly over standard setting). More important, competition is the only system that we believe is capable of diluting the role of political influence in standard setting. That is because, in a competitive environment, standard setters would have to satisfy investors as well as reporting firms and their auditors for their standards to have relevance in the marketplace and, hence, be adopted by companies.

Other forms of standards competition may be more politically feasible than either of the versions of controlled competition, although each would sacrifice some of its benefits. One alternative approach—*constrained competition*—would allow firms to choose their reporting standard only after some greater degree of harmonization has occurred between IFRS and U.S. GAAP. In effect, this approach encapsulates the goal of the harmonization effort that the IASB and the FASB announced in September 2002. A variation of constrained competition, which could be labeled *limited competition,* would allow companies to choose between the two principal standards but require the companies to reconcile "material" differences between the two standards (this would still amount to fewer reconciliations than the complete reconciliation that the SEC currently requires).

A final form of competition—albeit quite limited in form and effect— is *mutual recognition of accounting standards* by countries, rather than by stock markets. In the wake of Enron, this option has been pressed hardest by some Europeans, who have urged the United States to drop its reconciliation requirement for foreign-listed firms who report under IFRS (or prevailing European GAAPs) in return for Europeans recognizing U.S. GAAP for U.S. firms listed on European exchanges. Under mutual recognition, corporations would not have to adopt other countries' standards for their shares to be listed on those countries' stock markets. Thus, mutual country recognition would place at least some greater competitive pressure on both the FASB and the IASB than exists now, since firms from Europe and other countries whose markets would be mutually recognized in the United States would not be forced to reconcile to U.S. GAAP and, thus, effectively adopt that standard.

On purely substantive grounds, we prefer our first option—controlled competition—to any of the less ambitious alternatives just outlined, for the simple reason that only through greater competition in standard setting are the flaws in the monopoly model most likely to be corrected. Moreover, if competition is truly effective, it should not be held in suspense while the IASB and the FASB attempt to iron out the differences between their two sets of standards. To the contrary, if competition has merit—and we believe it does—then it would be better for the two sets of standards to remain different rather than gravitate toward one another.[18]

At the same time, we recognize that policymakers in the United States and elsewhere may be reluctant to embrace even the controlled competition approach we advocate here, for fear that it might lead to some loss in transparency arising from investors having to interpret financial reports prepared under different sets of standards. We believe that any such fear is overstated, however. As we have already argued, even under a single set of standards, firms have discretion in reporting their results, which means that investors do not now have the ability to make apples-to-apples comparisons that advocates of the current system may believe are possible. Moreover, under a regime of competitive standards, private sector analysts would have strong commercial incentives to translate or reconcile reports prepared under different standards.

Admittedly, in the absence of a full reconciliation requirement, analysts would not have access to all of the information required to make totally accurate translations of financial results from one standard to the other, unless firms voluntarily provided the requisite data. But estimated reconciliations are still likely to be of use to investors. And corporations would provide the requisite data for more complete reconciliations if the markets rewarded them for doing so.

Two other objections might be lodged against a competition in standards. One claim might be that the "market" for accounting standards, like the one for operating systems in personal computers or for videocassettes, is a natural monopoly. If this were true, it is conceivable that meaningful competition would be short-lived, resulting in a single winning standard. Such an outcome is indeed possible, but that is not an argument against running a competitive race in the first instance and, in the process, realizing the benefits from that competition while it lasts. In any event, it is not at all clear that competition in accounting standards would reduce to monopoly.

A final possible quarrel with standards competition is that accounting standards could become increasingly irrelevant, as individual investors and analysts equip themselves with tools to manipulate company financial data in any fashion they desire. We discuss this possibility in the next chapter, but conclude that for now and the foreseeable future, substantial numbers of investors and other users of financial statements (such as governments) will want standardized financial reporting. As long as that is true, standards will remain important, and by implication, so will some form of competition.

Enforcement

However much accounting standards may be perfected, investors will not be protected if the standards are not properly enforced. In light of the rising numbers of auditing problems in recent years, culminating with Arthur Andersen's widely publicized failures with respect to its audits of Enron, Waste Management, WorldCom, Qwest, and some other large well-known corporations, attention has properly been focused on how best to improve the verification of financial statements by auditors. There are two basic, somewhat overlapping, approaches to improving enforcement, which are not mutually inconsistent and ideally should be reinforcing: improved monitoring or oversight of the auditors themselves; and better (and more finely calibrated) incentives for those who conduct audits to carry them out properly. The Sarbanes-Oxley Act of 2002 contains both types of provisions, some of which we applaud. We have reservations about others, however.

Monitoring

The accounting debacles of recent years exposed the inadequacies in the previous system of overseeing the auditing profession: a combination of self-regulation (and audit standard setting) by the American Institute of Certified Public Accountants, suspension or removal of CPA certificates by the states that grant them, and supervision by the SEC. There is too much self-interest at the AICPA and its penalties are not credible, state efforts have lacked resources and expertise, and the SEC has been remiss in fulfilling its oversight obligation.

Soon after the Enron situation came to light, a consensus quickly emerged that the solution to this problem was to create a new independent body, monitored by the SEC, that would register and inspect all accounting firms that audit public companies; set and enforce auditing standards; and investigate and discipline accounting firms for misconduct. After some debate over its powers and how its members would be chosen, Congress established the Public Company Accounting Oversight Board. The board is to consist of five members, chosen by the SEC, who serve five-year overlapping terms; no more than two members may be or have been CPAs. Funding will be supplied by an assessment on all publicly held companies, based on their market capitalizations (except that the cost of registering public accounting firms and reviewing their annual reports will be financed by fees on those firms).[19] All of these costs, though, ultimately will be borne by shareholders. The oversight board has the authority to suspend or revoke an accounting firm's registration and can bar any person from associating with an accounting firm. The board can impose civil penalties of up $100,000 a person and $2 million an entity, if the misconduct is not intentional; for intentional misconduct, the penalties can be as high as $750,000 a person and $15 million an entity.

Although the oversight board was given the ability to improve monitoring of the auditing profession, its effectiveness will depend largely on the prowess of its chairman. The board unfortunately did not get off to a good start. Shortly after the Sarbanes-Oxley Act was passed, SEC chairman Harvey L. Pitt became embroiled in a series of controversies over the choice of the chairman that ultimately led to his resignation. Pitt's choice for the chairmanship of the board, William Webster, former director of the Central Intelligence Agency, also withdrew. When this book went to press in early 2003, a new SEC chairman had been named (William Donaldson), but a new chairman of the oversight board had not been chosen. Whether the board, when finally constituted, will be able to rise above the initial cloud that has settled upon it remains to be seen.

In any event, we remain skeptical that a new agency was needed at all. The SEC already had authority to discipline auditing firms that do not live up to their professional responsibilities. To be sure, the agency perhaps lacked the resources and personnel to fulfill this mandate properly, but more funding could easily cure this problem. (The agency did receive additional funding in fiscal year 2003, but not for oversight of the auditing profession.) Indeed, in the wake of the controversy over the agency's funding level for fiscal year 2003—and the mysterious, if not disappointing, failure of the Bush administration to back substantially more resources for the beleaguered and short-staffed agency—additional SEC funding should remain a top priority for future Congresses.[20] In addition, had no oversight board been created, Congress could have given the SEC additional statutory authority to impose more calibrated penalties, such as fines, rather than having to rely on such "nuclear weapons" as barring an offending auditing firm from certifying statements of public companies altogether (a penalty the commission understandably has been reluctant to impose).

Other arguments against having the SEC carry out functions that were delegated to the oversight board also lack merit. For example, it cannot be credibly claimed that the job of overseeing auditors is more complex than overseeing the stock exchanges, investigating fraud or insider trading, approving or disapproving proposed stock exchange rules, or carrying out the rest of the commission's statutory agenda. If the reason for creating an independent oversight board was to shelter it from political interference, then that argument, too, should not have been decisive. The SEC has effectively contracted out the setting of accounting standards to the FASB, but that has not prevented affected interests from influencing what the FASB does. In fact, precisely because enforcement is an inherent government police function that is carried out elsewhere by other federal agencies (such as the Department of Justice), Congress quite properly exercises its oversight responsibilities over those enforcement efforts. It would be no different if the SEC were to oversee the auditing profession directly.

But this is not what Congress has chosen to do (or what President Bush proposed). A new body will now oversee the auditing profession. It will report to the SEC, and it should have adequate funding from fees imposed on SEC-registered corporations and independent public accountants above those already collected by the U.S. Treasury from SEC registrants. Given the intense media interest in the accounting scandals reported during 2002, the new oversight board is likely to be operating under the harsh glare of public scrutiny for some time to come. For this reason alone, there is some reason to be optimistic that it will take its job seriously, regardless of who is chosen to be its chairman. How long this commitment will last—assuming it materializes—remains to be seen.

Better Incentives

Putting the equivalent of more and better "cops on the beat" is not the only way to improve auditing. Harnessing incentives is just as important, if not more so, because it may be cheaper and more effective than overseeing a profession whose very job is to oversee others.

One might view the responsibility for accurate financial reporting as a series of concentric circles, with the inner circle consisting of management, followed by audit committees of boards of directors and the board as a whole, auditors, and overseers of auditors (such as the new oversight board). Public policy should be designed to ensure that each of these layers, or gatekeepers, performs its functions with adequate care.

Begin with management. In enacting the Sarbanes-Oxley Act of 2002, Congress included a series of provisions aimed at ensuring that corporate managers—specifically chief executives—report the financial condition of their companies fairly. These include a new requirement that CEOs certify that the company financial statements "fairly present, in all material respects, the [company's] operations and financial condition" (a requirement also adopted by the SEC and implemented on August 14, 2002); a batch of new criminal penalties (with prison sentences of up to twenty-five years) for deliberate wrongdoing; and a provision requiring CEOs to repay any earnings-based bonuses if companies have to restate their earnings.

Although these provisions increase the incentives for CEOs to have their corporations report their financial conditions and performance fairly, in several important respects the provisions fall short of the mark. In our view, the effectiveness of the CEO certification provision is questionable over the long run, because CEOs will seek insurance (at company expense) to cover their liability. In the short run, however, the oath appears to have triggered a wave of caution, although many CEOs did not initially comply.[21] Similarly, while the new criminal penalties may allow policymakers to claim credit for disciplining wayward CEOs and their boards, we suspect that in the end there is less to this reform than meets the eye. The reason: convicting high-level executives of accounting fraud is very difficult under the best of circumstances. The issues in such trials tend to be highly technical, and the defendant executives can point to the discretion that even U.S. GAAP (let alone IFRS) necessarily permits firms and their auditors. Moreover, prosecutors must prove that the defendants had a clear intent to commit fraud and prove it beyond a reasonable doubt. These are high hurdles to jump. Thus, while federal prosecutors already have brought high-profile criminal cases against top executives of some of the firms whose accounting misdeeds have been in the news (such as the officers of

Adelphia and Enron), and in some cases have obtained successful plea agreements, we would be surprised if more than a relatively few executives will land behind bars. Consequently, the ultimate deterrent impact of the new criminal penalties is far from clear.

We are somewhat more sanguine about the likely effectiveness of the requirement that chief executives sacrifice their bonuses if earnings must be restated. This strong monetary disincentive should make CEOs think twice about using overly aggressive accounting, and regulators can impose it without the need to show intent or gross negligence (as is the case in criminal or civil cases for fraud) or even simple negligence. Corporate officers still can avoid some monetary liability, however, by taking advantage of state bankruptcy laws. In particular, the laws of Texas and Florida allow bankrupts to shelter their personal residences, regardless of the economic values of those residences, from creditors, court judgments, or fines. Pensions also are protected. Hence, corporate officers who plan sufficiently well could still keep a large portion of ill-gotten gains. And then there is the time-honored device of moving money offshore. We suspect that a number of executives may take this course in an effort to shelter their assets should the authorities really attempt to make them disgorge their bonuses.

We would be more optimistic about shifting incentives for U.S. corporate officials in the proper direction if the FASB soon required all stock options, especially those granted to high-level executives, to be expensed. We suspect that expensing would mitigate the use and extent of stock option grants, and thereby reduce some of the incentives that some executives now have to misstate or smooth earnings in an effort to keep their stock prices up and thus enhance the value of their stock options. Fortunately, the IASB already has proposed that the cost of stock options be expensed, which should provide the appropriate incentives for managers of corporations in European countries and other nations that have adopted IFRS. As for the United States, there is at least some prospect that the new NYSE and NASDAQ listing rules, which require shareholders to approve executive compensation packages, will reduce the size of those packages and thus perhaps reduce some of the incentives that some corporate officials may now have to manage their companies' earnings.[22]

The board of directors is the next line of defense in ensuring appropriate disclosure. Board members should have strong incentives to fulfill their responsibilities as agents of the shareholders. Yet, too often corporate boards have consisted of members handpicked by the corporate CEOs and thus have lacked independence. This state of affairs should change now that both the NYSE and the NASDAQ have amended their listing requirements to require that a majority of board members be independent of management. Furthermore, the exchanges now require all members of the nominating and compensation committees of corporate boards to be independent.[23] These measures should enhance the board of directors' role as monitors and evaluators of the senior managers' performance.

The audit committee of the board of directors, in particular, plays a direct and vitally important role in monitoring the internal accounting of a corporation and the work of its external auditor. We applaud the provision of the Sarbanes-Oxley Act of 2002 requiring all members of audit committees to be independent directors and giving them the sole power to hire and fire the external auditors. The law also requires corporations to give audit committees full support to hire independent attorneys and other experts to fulfill their duties.

The new listing rules of the NYSE strengthen board audit committees—appropriately in our view. Specifically, the rules require external auditors and the internal auditors to meet with the audit committee at specified times without the presence of the company's senior managers. The rules also preclude the members of the audit committee, unlike other board members, from taking any part of their board compensation in stock options; instead, audit committee members must be paid in cash or stock.

Because members of the boards of directors and their audit committees are subject to lawsuits should they appear to fail to fulfill their fiduciary responsibilities, they should have strong incentives to evaluate the financial reports produced by management and the extent to which their corporation's internal and external auditors have done their jobs. Still, there are reasons for caution. Despite the new rules, even "independent" directors may be less independent than they might appear. For example, directors might fear losing their compensation if they upset the CEO, or they may not have the time or expertise to evaluate the fairness of the financial reports. They usually rely, instead, on the evaluation by external auditors.

External audit firms of independent public accountants also have strong incentives to perform their jobs and to protect their reputations. After all, their "product" is a combination of professional expertise and the belief by users of financial statements that they attest only to financial statements that present the financial condition of a firm in accordance with GAAP. If external auditing firms even appear to be seriously remiss in performing their responsibilities, they can expect to be sued. Consequently, they certainly care about their liability exposure. Just ask the partners of Andersen, who face potentially huge liability costs over and above the amounts that their insurer may cover. Or ask the partners of any of the other accounting firms who must fear that the same thing could happen to them and who probably will now incur greater insurance costs.

The failures of previously respected accounting firms to prevent their clients from violating basic, GAAP-enshrined rules, such as proper revenue and expense recognition, have led many to question the effectiveness of liability-based incentives, however. Some observers have suggested that legal changes reduced potential liability penalties sufficiently to remove auditors' concerns about being suborned by clients. As we suggested in the last chapter, however, this tempting explanation does not appear to be supported by the facts.

We suggest, though, that one important reason for the audit failures is inadequate punishment of individual CPAs who attested to seriously misleading financial statements. The problem, we believe, is that the liability and enforcement system of the past has concentrated largely on deterring auditing *firms*, but *not individual audit partners*, from negligence or deliberate wrongdoing.

This is not the conventional view, at least as it has been so far reflected in the public arena or in the halls of Congress, where auditor responsibility has been debated and now been addressed. In particular, the Sarbanes-Oxley Act implicitly blames past auditor failures on the extensive involvement of audit firms in nonaudit consulting businesses, which critics argued gave auditors undue incentives to compromise their audits in the hope of holding on to lucrative nonaudit business. The Andersen relationship with Enron has become something of a "poster child" for this claim: in the year before Enron's failure, Andersen earned more from Enron in consulting fees ($27 million) than in auditing fees ($25 million). A 2001 study by the SEC reports that nonaudit activities are widespread among auditing firms.[24]

By early summer of 2002, out of a desire to preserve the reputations of their audits, the four remaining large audit firms had taken steps either to sell off some of their nonaudit businesses entirely (notably, information technology consulting) or to forgo nonaudit work for their audit clients. The Sarbanes-Oxley Act subsequently wrote the concerns about the mixing of audit and nonaudit work into law by prohibiting outside auditors from reviewing any internal accounting and data processing work they may have carried out for an audit client and from providing a series of other specified services for an audit client. In addition, the law requires audit firms to obtain explicit permission from the SEC to engage in certain nonaudit businesses, such as tax and financial advice, and it further requires boards of directors to approve permissible nonaudit assignments given to audit firms. Collectively, these new requirements are likely to have the practical effect of prohibiting audit firms from providing any nonaudit services to their audit clients (although auditors may still provide nonaudit services to clients whose accounts they do not audit).

Although there is a compelling case for preventing auditors from reviewing the internal audit functions they conducted in the first place, we believe that the criticism of auditors being in other businesses and the related restrictions designed to divorce the two are misplaced. Even if confined to performing audit work for clients, auditors still face the prospects of losing that business if they displease their clients. As a result, audit firms that are intent on keeping their clients at virtually all cost are likely to have the same incentives to compromise the quality of their work as they allegedly did before.[25] This problem should be cured by the new requirements prohibiting managers from hiring and firing auditors, but as discussed shortly, this prohibition only underscores the fact that it is the hiring and firing decision that really matters for providing the right incentives for auditors, not whether auditors are engaged in nonaudit businesses for audit clients.[26]

Meanwhile, the restrictions on audit firms, coupled with the new stiff oversight of auditing by the oversight board, will increase the cost of audits. In addition, with the demise of Arthur Anderson, the Big Five have been reduced to the Big Four. The net result is that in light of the concentrated nature of the auditing industry, the additional costs of carrying out audits should increase audit fees. These higher fees necessarily will have to be paid by shareholders and consumers of the affected corporations' products. We question whether the savings to shareholders from presumably better audits will be sufficient to offset these costs, particularly considering that shareholders can hold a diversified portfolio of stocks that mitigates the effect of individually costly audit failures.

There are also reasons to be skeptical of another widely discussed proposal: requiring companies to rotate their external audit firms every several years. It is possible, of course, that some auditors who know they are going to be replaced and have their work scrutinized closely by a successor will be more careful in carrying out their work every year. But another effect may work in the opposite direction; once the rotation is over, auditors may tacitly promise lenient treatment in the "beauty contests" that firms would hold on a regular basis to choose their next auditor. Furthermore, if the audit restrictions have the effect of reducing the number of large audit firms, mandatory rotation of firms will look even less practical and promise even fewer benefits than its proponents expect. In the end, the Sarbanes-Oxley Act requires rotation only of the audit *partner* every five years (down from the previous seven) and asks the Government Accounting Office to study whether the firms themselves should be rotated. Elsewhere, the European Commission and Great Britain are studying the idea. Singapore already has mandatory rotation of audit firms, as does Italy (where we understand it is perceived as a failure).

Ultimately, mandatory rotation and the prohibition on nonaudit work address only the *symptoms* and not the true underlying problem revealed in recent audit failures: that auditors have had incentives to compromise the quality of their audits because their engagements have been determined by the same corporate managers who oversee the financial reports the auditors examine. When the U.S. securities acts were considered in the 1930s, one proposed "solution" to this potential conflict was to establish a federal government audit agency in the Federal Trade Commission that would be responsible for auditing corporations with publicly traded securities. This idea was rejected, in part because it would have required an enormous bureaucracy and in part because of vigorous opposition by the public accounting profession. There is every reason to believe that these same concerns and objections would prevail today.

Some have suggested more radical solutions that would shift the hiring and firing of auditors entirely to third parties such as the stock exchanges, the SEC, or even a company's liability insurer.[27] While superficially appealing, each of these alternatives presents numerous practical problems growing out of the fact that there are some 17,000 corporations with publicly traded shares that require audits. Some mechanism would have to be used to assign auditors to all of these companies: "beauty contests" for each assignment, or a bidding and auction system. Whatever the mechanism, a potentially large bureaucracy would be required to administer that process.

In principle, the cost and complexity could be reduced if the rights to audit numerous firms were auctioned off in a package. But in practice, how would the packages or groupings be constructed, and on what basis? To what extent would audit firms found guilty of negligence in one or more cases be restricted from bidding for the rights to other audits? And then there is problem of ensuring that no single auditing firm or a select grouping of firms smaller than the Big Four effectively corners the market for audit services. That problem might be solved by imposing market share limits, but doing so very likely would invite political interference into the auditor selection process (perhaps resulting in setaside programs that might not be in shareholders' interests).

In short, we believe the practical obstacles to assignment of auditors by third parties are simply too great. The incentive problems are better addressed instead through the provisions of the Sarbanes-Oxley Act requiring auditors to be chosen by audit committees and the new NYSE listing rules ensuring the independence of the members of those committees and changing the way they are compensated.

While policy has focused primarily on strengthening incentives for audit firms to act in shareholders' interest, more could be done to strengthen incentives for individual external auditors. As we point out in chapter 2, regulatory bodies have rarely disciplined CPAs who falsely or negligently attest to financial statements that do not substantially conform to GAAP. Consequently, we believe, more than a few CPAs have given in to the rewards from not displeasing a client. The creation of the auditing oversight board, which is charged with disciplining individuals as well as their firms, should improve this situation, provided the board takes its responsibilities more seriously than has the SEC, which all along has had the power to discipline individual accountants who falsely or negligently attest to financial statements filed with the agency. One further step that would be helpful would be to require the partner in charge of an audit and the confirming partner to sign their names to the audit report, as well as their firm's name. Such a measure would help ensure that individual auditors understand that they, as well as their firms, bear responsibility for audits.

Disclosure Enforcement in a Global Environment

Earlier we argued that although capital markets are becoming increasingly global in character, it is a mistake to believe that the world must therefore have a single set of accounting standards. Specifically, we claimed that some sort of competition best serves investors in standard setting, but that in any event even if policymakers agreed on a single standard, it very likely would fragment over time.

If a single set of accounting standards is something of a holy grail, then so is any effort to develop a common system across countries of *enforcing* accounting standards. As it is now, countries make different uses of the various institutions available for enforcing whatever accounting standards may exist—the liability system, regulation, market-based incentives, and the like. Given the differences in historical circumstances that have led to these institutional differences, countries are unlikely to make any serious effort to harmonize these differences anytime soon, although some limited efforts aimed at that result are under way. Shortly after the Sarbanes-Oxley Act was passed, American officials heard objections from around the world, but particularly from Europe, about the application of the law's requirements, especially its oversight of accounting firms doing business in the United States even when those firms are headquartered elsewhere. About a month before he resigned his post, former SEC chairman Pitt signaled that he was willing to consider exempting auditors from the European Union from the auditing oversight provisions, but only on the condition that the EU establish a system of oversight for auditors in its member countries that is similar to the one just created in the United States.

Still, major differences in enforcement measures will persist among countries. The more relevant question for those investors interested in comparability across countries, however, is whether the *results* of those different enforcement systems might somehow converge over time. That is, is it possible to provide investors with more assurances than they have now that the financial figures published in different countries, even though they may be prepared under different reporting conventions, have at least roughly the same degree of trustworthiness?

Before the Enron scandal broke, there was an effort within the accounting profession to accomplish this very objective. Under the auspices of the International Federation of Accountants (IFAC), a forum of thirty of the largest accounting firms in the world issued a proposal in September 2001 to establish a peer review system for periodically and randomly reviewing the audits by those firms of "transnational" companies. The aim of this proposal was to establish some uniformity in audit results, initially for companies doing business in different countries.

The forum exercise continues, but in the wake of the various accounting debacles in the United States, self-regulation appears to have been discredited, at least for the time being and in the form in which it was undertaken. Nevertheless, we believe that this effort should not be abandoned. Indeed, it should proceed as quickly as feasible, because independent auditors and their audit firms are sorely in need of a reaffirmation that they still maintain the probity and high professional standards with which they have long been identified.

We suggest, therefore, that the forum develop a set of ethical and professional standards of auditing and reporting to which all member firms would agree. These should emphasize that financial statements attested to by forum members adhere to generally accepted auditing standards that provide a high degree of certainty that the numbers reported in those statements present a fair and trustworthy view of a company's financial status and changes in that status over a period. The accounting standards to which the statements conform may be those promulgated by the United States, the European Union, or any other country whose standards are similar. Investors who use these statements could thus be assured that the contents of the statements are very likely to be what they purport to be.

The forum could ensure compliance by its members in two ways. First, peer reviews of randomly selected audits could be conducted. Second, if these reviews found that the audits failed to meet the auditing standards or that the numbers attested to were misleading because they violated key accounting conventions, the firms could be fined and the partners who supervised the audit and the confirming partners could be disciplined. In particular, member firms could pledge to dismiss partners who were found to have been seriously negligent. The firms also could require their audit and confirming partners to sign agreements stating that they had conducted their audits appropriately, and that if the forum found they did not, that they would abide by any forum sanctions. Such sanctions could be resignation or the payment of monetary damages.

In the meantime, until some organization like the forum develops and is widely accepted, investors will have to live with differences in enforcement regimes and their results. The fruitless search for true comparisons of the financial results of firms in different countries may continue. But if investors truly value greater harmonization in enforcement, then another way to deliver that result will be through competition among exchanges, assuming national governments allow it. Exchanges associated with high-quality accounting standards and enforcement should attract issuers and investors alike and take market share away from exchanges with less stellar records in both these areas. Policymakers should therefore give more serious attention to promoting competition among exchanges, since that may be an effective and practical way to bring about the greater harmonization in and reliability of reporting that investors appear to want.

Concluding Assessment

In designing remedies to the flaws in the current system of corporate disclosure—especially as they have been revealed by the wave of accounting scandals in the United States—it is important to address underlying problems and not symptoms. We have argued in both this chapter and the last that at least in the United States, the main problems lie in the way in which accounting standards are set and enforced.

Congress, the stock exchanges, and the markets have not fully addressed these problems. No one has yet satisfactorily addressed the flaws in the existing system for setting accounting standards. That will not be done in a productive fashion, in our view, until some degree of competition is introduced between standard-setting bodies—the FASB and the IASB in particular.

As for enforcement, U.S. policymakers have improved the monitoring of the auditing profession, while providing various new incentives—mostly in the form of penalties rather than positive incentives—for corporate officers, board members, and auditors to pay greater attention to preparing and publishing trustworthy financial statements. Some of these measures should work, while others may not or may even be counterproductive.

Finally, just as one set of accounting standards universally applicable throughout the world is an unlikely objective, so too is a single system of enforcement of accounting standards (or system of corporate governance, more generally). The nascent effort to ensure greater uniformity in enforcement results instead, through self-regulation by the auditing profession commenced before the Enron scandal broke, should be continued and strengthened because, if successful, it could benefit investors as well as auditing firms that insist on maintaining high audit standards. Still, investors will have to live with the fact that true comparability of financial statements reflecting firms' performance is an objective that may never be achieved.

4 | *Disclosure Challenges Ahead*

The continuing flow of accurate, relevant, and timely information is central to the functioning of capital markets. The accounting debacles of 2002 harshly reminded investors of this simple truth. When investors cannot trust the earnings figures companies publish, they fear buying stocks. And when buyers do not want to purchase, stock prices fall, as they did pretty much across the board during the summer of 2002, for this and other reasons.

The various accounting and auditing reforms that have already been implemented—through legislation, changes in listing requirements by exchanges, and investor pressure—should help restore investors' faith in financial statements, although, as we discussed in the last chapter, certain reforms may be unnecessary or counterproductive. However, even trustworthy earnings figures may be of limited value to investors interested in projecting the future cash flows of the companies in which they might invest. This is so for four reasons.

First, published financial reports inherently are backward-looking, especially so because assets and liabilities are usually recorded at historical costs.

They are not recorded at current market values because these numbers either are not available or cannot be determined objectively. To be sure, many analysts and investors use earnings reports, past trends in earnings, key ratios and other relationships, and other financial information to extrapolate into the future. They also use the information presented in financial reports to evaluate managers' performance. But as the market turmoil of 2002 has demonstrated once more, making projections solely on the basis of reported earnings can be very dangerous, since the future for many firms may not look at all like the past. In recent years, for many investors and journalists "the future" largely has become what the analyst community says it is, with firms under increasing pressure to hit or exceed analysts' earnings projections. In turn, this pressure has contributed to the widely derided practice of "earnings management," or the manipulation of reported revenues and expenses in ways that generate reported earnings that do not disappoint market—or more accurately, analysts'—expectations.

Second, much of the value the market assigns to many companies is *intangible* and cannot be found on their balance sheets (or income statements)—largely because intangible assets often cannot be bought and sold in the marketplace independent of the company itself. Intangible assets include not only intellectual property such as patents, copyrights, trademarks, and trade secrets, but also the value of a company's work force, its customer base, its name brand and recognition, advertising, and all other intangibles that contribute to its ability to generate earnings. Intangibles are important not only for so-called high-tech companies, but also for many "old economy" enterprises that may have unique production processes, valuable brand names, superior reputations for quality and service, highly trained work forces, and stable customer bases.[1]

How do we know that intangible assets are important, and increasingly so? Because the market values of companies (as shown by the prices of their shares) tell us so. In a study of intangibles, Baruch Lev calculated the ratio of market values to book values for the stocks in the S&P 500 Index and found that it had doubled, from 3:1 to 6:1, between the beginning and the end of the 1990s.[2] Although stock prices have fallen substantially since then, they remain well above the levels of even the mid-1990s, and so there is little doubt that market-to-book ratios have increased markedly over the past decade. Some of this difference probably is attributable to understated assets (such as the effect of inflation on buildings and inventory recorded as last-in, first-out), but much of it likely is the result of the market valuing assets that are not reported on the balance sheet—among them, the value of customers, employees, research and development, and other intangible assets.[3]

Third, some important nonfinancial information relevant to pricing the future is not reported in financial reports. Other important information may be reported only quarterly or annually (and even then with a substantial delay), although it is generated constantly. A few examples: the gain or loss of new customers, insider sales or purchases of the company's stock, changes in management, new patents, and changes in demand for the company's products. To its credit, the SEC in the aftermath of the Enron affair, has required that more such information be disclosed and more frequently than ever before. Better Internet usage may further enhance continuous reporting.

Fourth, the information that is reported may not be that which investors find most useful. Financial reports necessarily present summaries of a company's underlying records in standard formats. As conditions change, these summaries and formats may no longer be (if they ever were) sufficiently meaningful windows through which a company's operations can be understood and its future prospects estimated. Nor are they likely to be sufficient for analysts to answer specific questions. The development of new computer-based technologies, especially the Internet, may soon make it possible, though, for investors, on their own or through independent advisers, to reconfigure company-specific information so that they need not rely on the GAAP-based financial statements that companies now produce.

Of special significance is the development of a new computer language, XBRL.[4] Based on another, more general language, XML, the new XBRL allows firms to place "tags," or identifiers, on all kinds of financial and non-financial information recorded in their databases. With these tags, users can extract firm-provided data and manipulate and rearrange them in any manner that they find useful. As we explain shortly, this is not possible with the current HTML-based text that companies now release on the Internet, largely because it is fixed and therefore cannot be rearranged.

The critical challenge now confronting firms, their accountants, the investing public, and policymakers is to define those steps that should be taken to provide the markets with more useful, relevant information that improves the ability of all market participants to make more accurate judgments about the future prospects of individual firms. The more effective that process is, the more efficient capital markets will be in allocating funds to those companies that most deserve it, while reducing the costs of raising capital for all those firms that need it.

What to Do with Intangibles

One natural response to the growing importance of intangible assets might be to require firms to put values on these assets and record them on their balance sheets. Perhaps even more ambitiously, firms could be asked to estimate how those values might increase or deteriorate over time, with the changes reflected in income statements. Indeed, corporations contemplating acquisitions or mergers should and probably do make such estimates about target firms.

It is one thing to make these valuations for internal business reasons; it is quite another to formally report estimates of intangible values in financial statements. The key difference lies in the fact that there are few, if any, organized markets for intangible assets. Accordingly, firms and—even more important in light of the recent accounting scandals—their auditors have no objective way to verify these values unless the assets are purchased, or valued at cost. In the absence of market values, firms would have to value intangible assets by using uncertain and readily manipulated estimates of expected cash flows and the interest rates at which these flows would be discounted. Furthermore, estimating the externality value of intangibles— their value in use within a firm compared to their value in exchange if they were to be bought and sold in a market—is very difficult and often impossible. For all these reasons, we believe that requiring firms to record the values of all intangible assets on their balance sheets—beyond those assets for which there are readily determined market values—not only would be costly, but potentially quite dangerous.

A more productive course is for firms to disclose more *nonfinancial* information that could help investors and their analysts indirectly appraise the value of intangibles. Examples include measures of consumer and worker satisfaction, product or service quality, successful innovation, education and

experience of the work force and management, and a variety of other indicators that, individually or collectively, often can shed far more light for
investors on the future ability of firms to generate earnings or cash flow
than can GAAP-based financial reports.

If all of this information is potentially so useful, why don't firms routinely disclose it now? There appear to be several reasons.

For one thing, no standards currently exist for deciding which measures
should be publicized or how the results should be computed and presented.
This problem is complicated by the fact that the appropriate measures
probably vary by industry.

Second, companies may have concerns that if they start releasing what
is now viewed to be unconventional data or information, they will be
locked into releasing it consistently in the future, because the market will
expect it. They also have reason to fear that release of such information
could create new risks of liability for alleged faulty disclosure. Some companies may also fear that the release of this information could assist their
competitors.

Although these various fears have some basis, they could be alleviated
through a careful standard-setting exercise, but one that takes account of
the fact that appropriate nonfinancial measures of current and likely future
financial health vary by industry (although some measures should be relevant to all industries). It is expecting too much, however, for industry trade
associations or their more generic equivalents (such as the Business Round-
table or the Chamber of Commerce) spontaneously to develop industry-
specific measures. Firms and their industries need a push by some third
party. The FASB has a project in this area and its participation is welcome.
But there may be limits to what the FASB can do, because the main job of
the board is to set *financial* reporting standards; historically it has not
addressed the reporting of nonfinancial information (although it has sponsored research in the area). More important, the FASB is extremely busy
with other projects, especially its planned overhaul of U.S. GAAP, and may
not have the time or resources to sponsor or organize the series of industry-
specific forums that we believe are necessary to help design appropriate
nonfinancial indicators.

Accordingly, we recommend that the SEC—and its equivalents in other
countries—assume this role, not through any formal rulemaking process,

but as a convener of industry-specific and more generic cross-industry forums. Initially, the purpose of these meetings should be to identify useful nonfinancial indicators, which the media could help publicize. Over time, we believe there is a reasonable chance that investors, especially large institutional investors, would begin to demand that the firms whose shares they purchase publish how they are performing by these measures. At some point, thereafter, regulators or standard-setting bodies might mandate the publication of those indicators the market has made most popular.

The forums we advocate can and should build on the forward-looking thinking about nonfinancial measures that has already taken place, illustrated by the list in the accompanying box. Possible indicators began to appear in the literature in the early 1990s, when the FASB, led by its then-chairman Edward Jenkins, issued a report on the subject.[5] Others have since followed suit.[6] Most recently, the Organization for Economic Co-operation and Development has launched an effort to identify useful nonfinancial indicators to measure company performance.[7]

External auditors should participate in these discussions so that they can develop and propose guidelines that would allow them to audit the additional information, if this service is demanded by the corporations. Such audits would give users reason to believe that the numbers are trustworthy and, hence, more useful to them.

Serious consideration should also be given to shielding corporations that make additional information available from lawsuits by attorneys and the investors they presumably represent, by instituting a "safe harbor" provision. Corporations and independent auditors should be liable only where gross negligence in calculating, presenting, and auditing the numbers can be demonstrated by plaintiffs.

In any event, it is much too early to think about mandating the disclosure of specific nonfinancial indicators, whether generically or by industry. Time is needed for experimentation. But the process should begin.

Disclosure and the Internet

A second policy challenge is how best to harness the power of technology—computers and the Internet—to facilitate more complete and more

---

Possible Nonfinancial or Nontraditional Indicators of Performance

Following are some nonfinancial and nontraditional indicators of performance that have been proposed by various experts as potentially valuable information to include in financial reports.

Percentage of sales from developed in last x months

Average time to bring a new idea to market

Market's perception of quality of product

Market's perception of quality of service

Percentage (or number) of customers accounting for x percent of sales

Customers' industry concentration

Percentage (or number) of suppliers accounting for x percent of purchases

Suppliers' industry concentration

Age of units being replaced

Customer reorder rates

Percentage of revenue from new products

Elapsed time from raw materials to finished goods

Breakeven time (time required to recover development costs)

Sources: Robert K. Elliott, "The Third Wave Breaks on the Shores of Accounting," *Accounting Horizons*, vol. 6, no. 2 (1992), pp. 61–85; and Robert K. Elliott and Peter D. Jacobson, "Costs and Benefits of Business Information Disclosure," *Accounting Horizons*, vol. 8, no. 4 (1994), pp. 80–96.

Rejection rate for products

Patents obtained annually

Number of design installation contracts received

Ratio of contracts awarded to number of proposals

Market share (current and over time)

Product development lead time

Source: Jenkins Report, American Institute of Certified Public Accountants, *Improved Business Reporting—Customer Focus* (www.aicpa.org/members/div/accstd/ibr/appiv.htm, February 21, 2000)

---

rapid corporate disclosure. We are not the first to address this challenge, and we suspect we will not be the last.[8] But we have some views on the subject that may not (yet) be widely shared, but that we hope are nonetheless useful.

So far, in the disclosure realm, the Internet has been primarily, if not exclusively, nothing more than a faster and more convenient medium for transmitting corporate information to the public. Essentially, the same information that firms disclose in written form is now also posted on the

Financial drivers: sales growth rate, operating profit margin, cash tax rate, working capital to sales, capital expenditures to sales, and cost of capital

Research and development productivity (number of patents per R&D dollar)

Size of new product pipelines

Strength of company's brands relative to competitors

Ranking in cross-industry benchmarking studies

Source: PricewaterhouseCoopers, *Value Reporting Forecast, 2000* (New York, 1999).

Revenue and gross margins from new products

Percentage of revenues from new customers, market segments, or geographic regions

Percentage growth of business with existing customers

Number of responses to solicitations, or the conversion rate at which customers responding to solicitations actually purchase goods or services

Solicitation cost per new customer acquired, or new customer revenues per dollar of solicitation cost

Breakeven time (time for new product to cover development cost)

Source: Robert S. Kaplan and David P. Norton, *The Balanced Scorecard* (Boston: Harvard Business School Press, 1996).

We are indebted to Peter Wallison for compiling this list.

web, including press releases, annual reports, and other company publications. In addition, the Internet is used effectively as a substitute for a conference call when company officials "webcast" their quarterly "analysts' calls," or sessions in which officials elaborate on their quarterly earnings releases and answer questions from analysts about them.

The Internet nonetheless can provide even faster and more complete disclosure than is the case now, in two ways. First, it can serve as the distribution mechanism for financial reports released even more frequently than quarterly—say, monthly, and eventually perhaps even at shorter intervals (approaching something close to real-time disclosure). Most companies already routinely prepare revenue and expense reports for internal purposes at more frequent intervals than every ninety days. Indeed, financial institutions—banks, securities firms, and mutual fund companies—typically close their books *every night*. Why not then consider ways to speed up the communication to investors of financial information that is already in companies' possession and thereby level the playing field between corporate insiders, shareholders, and potential shareholders?

More frequent financial disclosure may also help address the nagging problem of earnings management. Managers manipulate their companies' income statements, it is commonly alleged, in order to meet analysts' projected quarterly earnings targets. If, however, companies routinely reported their financial results much more frequently than every quarter, analysts would have to develop earnings forecasts more frequently than on a quarterly basis, and the perceived importance of the "correctness" of the forecasts would most likely diminish. Thus, more frequent reporting could reduce incentives of managers to manipulate earnings (and auditors to overlook it) to meet or beat each of the analysts' forecasts.[9]

Another possible outcome is that more frequent disclosures would put more emphasis on cash flows, and less on such noncash items as depreciation, amortization, and the like. Since fundamental stock valuation ultimately rests on projections on future cash flows, this would be a salutary development.

One objection to more frequent disclosures of financial information is that the data necessarily would be unaudited. But as it is now, quarterly financial data are unaudited and will remain that way unless or until regulators come up with guidelines for limited, cost-effective audits of more frequently reported data. Once those guidelines are developed, it would be appropriate to grant firms a safe harbor from liability if they comply. In the meantime, *mandating* more frequent reporting at this point is premature. Many firms simply may not be able to comply with such a requirement, even for reporting monthly, let alone more frequently.

The second technology-related challenge is to find ways of using the Internet not only as a medium for transmitting information but also as a vehicle for disclosing and aggregating data in ways that investors find useful. Here is where the XBRL project comes in.

Currently, information available on websites is written in HTML, which is essentially a set of instructions to a display mechanism (a monitor or printer) on how to show a document. HTML generally does not permit the user to identify, extract, manipulate, or rearrange individual items of data, such as the name of a financial account or the amount that is in it. In contrast, XML permits the tagging of individual "data elements," and thus allows the users to rearrange or manipulate them. For financial analysis in particular, XML could allow users to download data from a website into, say, a spreadsheet program. The data could then be used, perhaps with other information, to form a table, graph, or any other representation that provides users with greater insights than they could obtain from the statements prepared and publicly distributed by a company.

The XBRL project, an application of XML, was set up by the American Institute of Certified Public Accountants. More than 170 companies worldwide have so far joined the consortium. Together with some of the major standard setters around the world, including the IASB, these companies are developing a common financial language by using XBRL to tag all kinds of industry-specific data.[10] Users will know that one acronym stands for "cash," another for "accounts receivable," and so on. Once the XBRL-based tags are fully developed and implemented by companies, not only sophisticated financial analysts but a wide range of users will easily be able to take very detailed data from companies and reconfigure it in multiple ways, using widely available spreadsheet programs. In addition, XBRL will make it possible for companies to easily rearrange their own data in a variety of formats for multiple purposes including filings to regulatory authorities, stock exchanges, banks, contract partners, and auditors.

Some experts believe that once XBRL tags are widely available, users will be unchained from having to take financial data in the standardized formats in which they now appear. Thus, for example, users who want to develop a specialized indicator of a company's cash flow could do so simply by using the appropriate data elements in the company's income statement. Or investors who want to know how different assumptions about depreciation or amortization schedules might affect income could have their answers with a little manipulation in a spreadsheet. The possibilities for such rearrangement using XBRL are endless, although they are necessarily restricted to the data that companies choose to tag and publish.

Some observers have gone so far as to predict that XBRL could eventually make many of the current accounting standards as embodied in national GAAPs or IFRS eventually irrelevant. We see no inconsistency, however, between the appetite of investors and analysts for manipulating data in XBRL format and the continued desire of many of the same parties, as well as others, for having financial information presented in standardized formats. If nothing else, users are likely to want to compare their own formats with those more widely in use. Thus, we believe that projections of the imminent demise of at least the two most popular reporting conventions, U.S. GAAP and IFRS, are premature.

Instead, we believe that XBRL, if it proves successful, will reduce barriers to entry into the independent analysts' industry, while lowering costs for buy-side analysts. The major losers from XBRL are likely to be sell-side analysts, or those who work for investment banks. In effect, XBRL removes much of the mystery surrounding their work, enabling third parties and investors themselves to perform with ease much, or all, of the data manipulation that used to be the province of sell-side analysts.

Skeptics will question whether third-party analysts will survive in a marketplace where there is scant evidence that investors are willing to pay for investment advice. Apart from such independent analysts as Value Line, and a variety of stock newsletters, the independent analysts' industry has been marked by a shortage of competitors, all for a very simple reason: the customer demand has not been there. All of this could change, however, now that the reputations of sell-side analysts have been so severely battered, not just by the Enron affair, but by the collapse of the high-tech and telecommunications sectors where several high-profile sell-side analysts had once made their mark.

Investors have become painfully aware that the advice of some sell-side analysts was severely biased by the fact that, at least until recently, their compensation was tied to how much stock underwriting business they brought into their firms.[11] In the wake of the various accounting scandals of 2002, major investment banks and their trade association, the Securities Industries Association, have announced new policies barring this practice.

During the fall of 2002, major investment banks considered forming a new oversight body that, among other things, would require investment bank analysts to give their clients not only house-supplied research reports on specific companies, but also similar reports prepared by a number of independent analysts (a step of doubtful utility in our view).[12] For a time, it also appeared that either the SEC or the New York State Attorney General's office (which has led a number of high-profile investigations into potential abuses by research analysts affiliated with investment banks) might go further and actually force investment banks to divest their research operations.

Whatever measures ultimately are adopted to address the conflicts posed by sell-side investment bank research analysts, it is not clear to us whether these analysts will ever recover their reputations. This possibility should create a window of competitive opportunity for independent analysts to generate some business. Indeed, we would not be surprised to see some of the better analysts who now work for investment banks gradually leave their employers to establish their own firms. The market then would do the divesting, not the regulators. The key, though, is that if third-party firms, however they are formed, deliver something that investors value—and XBRL should help them do it—they should survive and prosper. If the firms do not supply something of value, they will die.

A related development might be the increased use of analysts by pension and mutual funds, the buy side of the market. In the past, the actual cost of securities analysis was buried in the transactions fees institutional investors paid to securities brokers and dealers, which allowed them to avoid having to report the cost as an operating expense. Considering the substantial losses many funds absorbed from their investments in Enron, WorldCom, and other firms that were touted by sell-side analysts almost to the day that they went under, the buy side of the market may now decide that it would be cost effective to do its own analysis, which would increase the demand for XBRL-accessed data.

Meanwhile, the SEC (and its counterparts elsewhere) should be out front in promoting the use of XBRL, not only to further enhance the role of independent analysts, but also to arm investors themselves with new tools for performing their own investment analysis. Securities regulators could give an informal blessing to the XBRL consortium and its efforts.

Regulators also might use their current electronic filing requirements to push the implementation of XBRL. For example, the SEC now requires public companies to file their financial statements in its EDGAR system, while regulators in the EU are discussing the formation of a similar system. With such systems in place, eventually regulators might require all electronic filings to be in XBRL. Indeed, Austria has proceeded down that path, allowing its companies to make their filings in XML formats. The Federal Deposit Insurance Corporation in the United States has gone further, requiring all banks to file their financial statements in XBRL by the end of 2003, while Australian authorities have issued the same requirement for all financial services companies by the end of 2002. And a major impulse for XBRL use is expected if fiscal authorities adopt it for tax return filings.

Finally, it is worth considering why regulators need to be involved at all in encouraging, and very tentatively mandating, the changes we have just discussed. If faster reporting, with data elements entered in XBRL formats, will help investors, then why shouldn't investor demand be sufficient to bring about the necessary degree of change?

One answer to this important question is that the benefits to investors from the changes we have described are, to some extent, "public goods." That is, the benefits are not easily confined to one or a few investors, but instead diffuse throughout the entire marketplace. As a result, the social good from faster and more user-friendly reporting, if it is cost effective, is greater than the private good. Like national defense, or a well-organized police force, improvements in reporting that benefit the capital markets as a whole need to be encouraged from institutions outside the marketplace, because investor demand alone is not likely to produce the optimal amount.

Of course, reasonable people can differ on whether the public good from better disclosure is greater or less than the costs to the companies of producing it and, if so, whether the net social benefits from mandating disclosure exceed the cost thereof. More research into the cost issue will be required before policymakers can be confident about getting too heavily involved in mandating the changes we have broadly suggested. Furthermore, freezing policy in one manner or another risks getting things wrong at the outset and thus frustrating constructive change down the road. That is also why we are cautious, suggesting that regulators put much of their emphasis on encouraging and facilitating market-driven developments, and less emphasis on mandates—at least for now.

Conclusion

There is more to fixing corporate disclosure than ensuring that more Enrons or WorldComs do not happen in the future. The current system rests on an accounting framework that is becoming increasingly insufficient to meet investors' demand for relevant information, especially information related to the intangible sources of value that are critical for so many firms.

The answer, however, is not to throw away the values that audited financial statements offer to investors. Although these financial statements do not and cannot provide all or even much of the information investors may want to make informed decisions, the statements have great value when the numbers they report are trustworthy. Shareholders and potential investors should be able to rely on these statements as valid reports of the managements' stewardship of the resources entrusted to them by shareholders. Balance sheets and income statements should report the financial condition at a particular date and its changes over a time period in accordance with rules that have not been manipulated by managers to cover up their failures and mislead shareholders and other users of the financial statements.

But what of investors' apparent demand for more current, more complete, and probably more meaningful information? Technology increasingly offers opportunities for disclosing information far more quickly and completely than in the past, including information that previously was unavailable, not easily used, or not able to be analyzed.

The next challenge for policymakers interested in improving the information system upon which the capital markets depend is to find ways to adapt and harness these new developments. It is a mistake to expect that policy will forever be ahead of new developments, anticipating which direction they will take. But policy also should not be in the business of frustrating constructive change. Toward that end, we have suggested here some modest initiatives that policymakers—specifically, securities regulators and their legislative overseers—could pursue to encourage developments already under way. These developments include promoting the development of nonfinancial indicators that may be as useful, if not more so, than conventional earnings figures in assisting investors to project future cash flows; encouraging the release of interim financial results, via the Internet, more frequently than every ninety days; and encouraging, possibly requiring, public firms to file their financial statements, prospectuses, and other relevant information in XBRL format in order to accelerate the use of XBRL by companies, investors, and analysts. Together, these measures can go a long way toward reducing some of the uncertainty investors now face. In the process, these steps will lower the cost of capital for all enterprises and enhance the efficiency of the capital markets.

Appendix:
What Are the Major Differences between GAAP and IFRS, and Why Do They Matter?

In chapter 3, we argued in favor of a competition in accounting standards—specifically between the Generally Accepted Accounting Principles set by the Financial Accounting Standards Board in the United States and the International Financial Reporting Standards established by the International Accounting Standards Board. The IASB is an outgrowth of the International Accounting Standards Committee, which was created in 1973 with the objective of developing standards that would be acceptable worldwide.

A major step toward worldwide use of the international standards was taken in 2000, when the International Organization of Securities Commissions recommended that its members permit multinational issuers to use IFRS for cross-border offerings and listings. More recently, the European Union moved to require listed corporations in its member countries to use IFRS as of 2005. Australia and Russia have both proposed that their listed corporations adopt IFRS by the same year. As a result of a major reorganization in 2001, the IASB is now actively seeking the convergence of national accounting standards and the IFRS. To this end, it has formed liaisons with leading national standard setters, including the FASB.

This appendix provides an overview of the major differences between U.S. GAAP and IFRS. While it is impossible to do full justice to the differences that exist in every detail to the two sets of standards,[1] we attempt in this appendix to give a flavor of the current principal differences, noting along the way some proposed changes in several standards that are intended to bring about convergence. Because several of the noted differences are optional—that is, because corporations may or may not choose to follow the particular standard—actual differences between the two sets of standards may, but need not, arise in practice.

Philosophical Differences

A broad, philosophical difference between IFRS and U.S. GAAP (and other national GAAPs) lies in their styles: IFRS is usually described as principles based, whereas U.S. GAAP is seen as rules based. While this distinction is overly simplistic, it does contain a kernel of truth because U.S. GAAP does contain many more detailed rules and guidance than IFRS. Furthermore, although U.S. GAAP leaves less room for individual judgment, some of the rules are inconsistent, largely because they have been promulgated at different times and even by different standard setters.

In contrast, principles-based standards contain broad guidelines and less specific, case-based guidance.[2] The application of principles requires more professional judgment than following detailed rules, however, and accordingly leaves room for interpretation.[3] In a highly litigious environment such as that in the United States, companies and their auditors face an increased litigation risk when they apply principles rather than rules.

U.S. GAAP is more voluminous than IFRS, because it contains specific details and guidance not only for special transactions, but also for many specific industries including financial institutions, insurance companies, business development and investment companies, mineral exploration, and the movie industry, among others. IFRS does not contain any industry-specific standards except one on disclosure for financial institutions. The IASB also is currently working on a standard for insurance contracts.

Lease Accounting

One popular criticism of the rules-based approach to accounting standards
is that it may provide incentives for companies to circumvent the spirit of
a rule by designing transactions specifically to avoid meeting its exacting
criteria. A classical example is lease accounting. Both IFRS and U.S. GAAP
currently follow similar accounting conventions and categorize lease contracts into capital leases and operating leases, based on the economic substance of ownership rights they provide rather than on who has legal ownership.[4] Capital leases are recognized in the financial statements of the
lessee, operating leases in those of the lessor.

U.S. GAAP provides detailed "bright line" guidance for leases, including quantitative criteria for capital leases, such as the notion that the risks
and benefits of ownership are deemed to have been transferred to the lessee
if the lease term is equal to 75 percent or more of the estimated economic
life of the leased property, and the beginning of the lease term does not fall
within the last 25 percent of the total economic life of the leased property.
If this or any of three other criteria is met, the lease must be recorded as an
asset with an equal liability. As a result, there is a propensity among U.S.
companies to structure lease transactions so that they qualify as operating
leases; that is, the items leased do not show up on the balance sheet as
recorded assets, but instead flow through the income statement to the
extent the lessee pays rental charges.

In contrast, the relevant international standard relies on a judgment
whether the lease transfers substantially all the risks and rewards incident
to ownership of the asset to the lessee, in which case the lessee recognizes
the asset. IFRS thus leaves the exact thresholds to management's discretion
(and auditors' judgment).

Consolidation

The Enron affair has illustrated how differences between principles-based
and rules-based approaches can matter. As we discuss in chapter 2, Enron
established many special purpose entities in such a way that they did not
meet the U.S. GAAP threshold (outside capital of less than 3 percent of

SPE assets) for consolidating the balance sheets of the SPEs with those of their sponsor. In so doing, Enron was able to push liabilities off of its balance sheet. Although the FASB has since considered revising that threshold (to 10 percent of assets), it has not changed the basic quantitative approach for deciding whether an entity should be consolidated.

Under IFRS, Enron would have had more difficulty avoiding consolidation, since the relevant broad principle requires a judgment as to whether an SPE is controlled in substance. That is determined by, among other criteria, whether the company retains the majority of the risks related to the SPE. Precisely because it requires corporate managers and their auditors to exercise judgment, IFRS also requires them to take more risk when presenting and opining about the financial affairs of a company and its possibly related enterprises. In the case of Enron, this approach might have discouraged the company or its auditors from excluding a number of the SPEs from its balance sheet.

Goodwill and Intangibles

Apart from the scope of consolidation, U.S. GAAP and IFRS differ greatly in their accounting treatment of goodwill arising from a business combination. The FASB fundamentally changed the accounting method of goodwill in 2001. It is now considered a nonwasting asset and consequently is not amortized systematically but instead is tested for impairment, at least annually. IFRS still requires goodwill to be amortized, generally over a maximum of twenty years. At this writing, the IASB is considering the adoption of an impairment-only approach for goodwill. Companies that use IFRS are pushing hard for this change, because it generally increases their earnings per share, as it did for U.S. companies. Of course, if the economy turns down and the value of goodwill is seen as impaired, reported earnings per share could be devastated.

A similar difference between the two sets of standards involves the accounting treatment of purchased intangible assets. If their useful life cannot be determined, the impairment-only approach is applicable under U.S. GAAP, but currently not under IFRS. The international treatment of intangibles, though, may move in the U.S. direction in the near future.

Mergers and Joint Ventures

The two sets of standards also display some difference when it comes to accounting for mergers. For the special case of a merger of equals, IFRS currently requires the pooling-of-interests method under which assets and liabilities are simply combined and any excess of the purchase price over the book values is charged against (reduces) equity, so that no fair-value revaluations and goodwill arise. The FASB has recently abandoned the pooling-of-interests method for U.S. GAAP and now requires corporations to account for all combinations as purchases. The assets and liabilities of the acquired firm are restated to market or fair values, and the excess of the purchase price over the restated assets less the restated liabilities is recorded as goodwill. The IASB is expected to follow suit.

As for joint ventures that are controlled by more than one company, U.S. GAAP accounts for them under the "equity method," which places on the asset side of each company's balance sheet only the investment it has in the enterprise, adjusted for its share of net income and reduced by distributions (dividends) accrued. IFRS permits a general option for proportionate consolidation, which essentially means that a fraction of the joint venture's assets are shown in the balance sheet of each company. U.S. GAAP also permits proportionate consolidation, but only if it is established industry practice, such as in some oil and gas ventures.

Research and Development Costs

There is a difference between the two standards for research and development costs. IFRS requires expensing of research costs but recognition of development costs if and when certain criteria are met. Under U.S. GAAP, all internally generated research and development costs must be expensed as they are incurred. However, computer software development costs are capitalized under U.S. GAAP after the technological feasibility of the software has been demonstrated (which also is a major criterion under IFRS to qualify for capitalization).

Fair-Value Accounting

In chapters 2 and 3, we criticized both sets of standards for moving in the direction of fair-value accounting. However, of the two standards, IFRS allows more fair-value measurements and is moving more rapidly in this direction than is U.S. GAAP. Under the international standards, however, the amounts by which operating assets (those not held for investment) are revalued are not included in the income statement but are carried directly to equity. This practice is an important limit on managers' incentives to overestimate fair values.

In particular, under IFRS, classes of property, plant, and equipment and (under highly restrictive circumstances) intangibles can be revalued to fair value. Revaluation must be made with sufficient regularity. Revaluation increases are credited directly to equity and circumvent the income statement totally, as they are not recycled upon disposal. Thus, they affect the balance sheet presentation of assets and liabilities, but not net income. Revaluations are popular in the United Kingdom, and many other EU member states also allow them.

In contrast, U.S. GAAP does not permit revaluation accounting and strictly requires historical cost for physical and intangible assets. However, in the United States, financial assets held for trading by investment and business development companies must be revalued to fair values, even where market values are not available. Hence, U.S. corporations can transfer nonfinancial assets to their subsidiaries in exchange for the subsidiaries' stock, transfer the stock (which now is a financial asset) to an investment-company subsidiary, and revalue the stock to fair value. Then, when the subsidiaries are consolidated with the parent, the nonfinancial assets, in effect, are revalued to fair values, and the changes in valuation are reported as income from investment-company operations.[5]

Another application of fair-value measurement relates to investment property, which is property held to earn rentals or for capital appreciation. Under IFRS, investment property can generally be measured at its fair value with changes in fair value included in income. In contrast, under U.S. GAAP, there are no specific rules for investment property accounting, but the general rules clearly do not allow for fair-value measurement.

Financial Instruments

The IFRS and U.S. GAAP standards for measuring financial instruments, including derivatives and hedge accounting, are currently not much different. Financial assets held to maturity are recorded at cost, while trading instruments and derivatives are recorded at fair value with gains and losses included in net income. Financial assets available for sale are valued at market value, but gains and losses are included directly in equity (other comprehensive income) under U.S. GAAP, whereas IFRS allows them to be included either in net income or in equity. Financial liabilities, except for trading liabilities, are measured at cost under both standards.

The IASB has recently published an exposure draft standard that includes an option to measure any financial asset and liability at full fair value by designating the financial instrument as held for trading.[6] The proposal moves in the direction of the draft standard of the international Joint Working Group on Financial Instruments, which at the end of 2000 proposed a fair-value measurement for all financial instruments including liabilities. However, for reasons discussed in chapters 2 and 3, we believe that the IASB's further embrace of fair values has significant potential for abuse.

Provisions and Contingencies

Less visible than any differences between the two standards regarding financial instruments are differences in the accounting for provisions and contingencies. Present obligations of uncertain timing or amount are recognized under IFRS if they are more likely than not to occur. They are measured basically using the statistical concept of expected value and are discounted. Under U.S. GAAP, recognition requires the probability of a contingent loss to be significantly greater than 50 percent; discounting generally is not allowed. While there is much room for judgment, as a general tendency U.S. GAAP permits fewer provisions and contingencies than does IFRS.

Stock Options

We criticize the accounting standard for employee stock options used in the United States because it does not require options, when granted, to be shown in the income and expense statement. Currently, no particular accounting treatment for share-based payments is prescribed under IFRS. Companies that use IFRS can select an appropriate method on their own and can apply the treatments that are applicable under U.S. GAAP. However, in late 2002, the IASB proposed a comprehensive standard that would require expensing of stock options, when granted.

Presentation

The differences between IFRS and U.S. GAAP regarding presentation of financial statements are noticeable. For example, under U.S. GAAP (and also under SEC rules) items on the balance sheet are presented in the order of declining liquidity. Under IFRS items are presented in two broad categories: current and noncurrent. U.S. GAAP and SEC rules require presentation of the income statement based on the "cost of sales" method, wherein the cost of sales is deducted from revenue to arrive at gross profit, and the expenses of other functions (such as distribution and administration) are then deducted. IFRS allows the use of the "nature of expense" method as an alternative, wherein expenses are aggregated into raw material, staff, depreciation, and the like, and then are deducted from revenue and changes in inventories. Presentation of discontinued operations differs between the two standards, as does the definition of unusual and extraordinary items. In an exposure draft released in May 2002, the IASB proposed to abandon the separate presentation of extraordinary items in the income statement altogether. Cash flow statements may differ due to differing classifications of interest, dividends, and income taxes under IFRS and U.S. GAAP.

Segment Reporting

The reporting of different business activities (or segments) of a corporation varies between IFRS and U.S. GAAP in the underlying approach and in the items that should be disclosed. IFRS, similar to former U.S. GAAP standards, follows a risks and rewards approach, which implies segmentations according to business and geographical characteristics. In contrast, U.S. GAAP adopts a management approach that bases segment reporting directly on the form and content of a company's internal reporting system. While segment reporting under IFRS tends to allow a better comparison of segments across companies, U.S. GAAP is preferable if one attempts to understand how management sees its operations.

Enforcement

Finally, as we discuss in this book, accounting standards are only as good as the enforcement infrastructure in which they are embedded. Thus, comparing standards literally does not fully capture their actual application in the business community. The IASB (similar to the FASB) does not consider enforcement of the standards it promulgates as its task, but that of national or supranational institutions.

Notes

Chapter One

1. "Badly in Need of Repair," *Economist*, May 4, 2002, pp. 66–68.

2. It is more than likely that the drop in stock prices had some adverse effects on the underlying real economy. For one set of estimates, see Carol Graham, Robert E. Litan, and Sandip Sukhtankar, "The Bigger They Are, The Harder They Fall: An Estimate of the Costs of the Crisis in Corporate Governance," Brookings Policy Brief (August 2000).

3. "Rebuilding Trust—Before It's Too Late," *Business Week*, June 24, 2002, p. 164.

4. The Sarbanes-Oxley Act of 2002 formally gave the FASB the authority to establish accounting and auditing standards, subject to oversight by the SEC; all publicly traded companies and public accounting firms must follow the standards. The act also created the Public Company Accounting Oversight Board, which is charged with overall supervision of registered public accounting firms, which public companies must use as their external auditors.

5. E. S. Browning, "Where Is The Love? It Isn't Oozing From Stocks," *Wall Street Journal*, December 24, 2001, p. C1.

6. "FASB Finally Comes Up with SPE Rules," *Treasury & Risk Management*, vol. 12, no. 7 (August 2002), p. 9.

7. As we discuss in chapter 3, this outcome could be achieved either directly (by having explicit rules allowing firms listing on exchanges to choose the reporting standards) or indirectly (by allowing exchanges, each having their own associated disclosure system, to compete in different countries without restriction).

8. A good case can be made, however, in support of mandatory rotation of auditing *partners* within the same firm, as is now required by the Sarbanes-Oxley Act of 2002.

Chapter Two

1. See, in particular, William Z. Ripley, *Main Street and Wall Street* (Boston: Little, Brown and Co., 1927).

2. As discussed in chapter 3, Congress and the stock exchanges moved in the summer of 2002 to ensure that corporate managers who were in a position to manipulate a firm's financial statements would not also be responsible for hiring and firing the firm's external auditors.

3. The AICPA has played a role in setting GAAP through its Accounting Standards Executive Committee's Statements of Operating Positions (SOP) and its industry audit guides, when these are accepted by the FASB. However, the AICPA has announced that in the future only the FASB will establish GAAP.

4. An important exception is fair-value accounting for financial assets, which we examine later.

5. A key example is the expense associated with stock options, which is not currently reported as an expense in the income statement. We address this issue later in the chapter.

6. For firms that might liquidate, transaction costs reduce the values of most assets usually below their purchase price.

7. Managers should also distinguish between revenue earned from the operations of the enterprise and income derived from the sale and revaluation of assets and liabilities. This distinction is important because many users of financial statements (particularly investors) base their calculations of a company's prospects on its past performance, as reflected by its revenue and net income from continuing operations.

8. At the time Enron declared bankruptcy, its reported assets were $63 billion. WorldCom reported assets of $107 billion when it went down. Until these two failures, the largest corporate collapse was Texaco, which had $36 billion in assets when it declared bankruptcy in 1987.

9. These restatements reduced previously reported net income to the following levels: 1997, $28 million (27 percent of previously reported $105 million); 1998, $133 million (19 percent of previously reported $703 million); 1999,

$248 million (28 percent of previously reported $893 million); and 2000, $99 million (10 percent of previously reported $979 million).

10. "Report of Investigation by the Special Investigative Committee of the Board of Directors of Enron Corp.," William Co. Powers, chair, Raymond S. Troubh, and Herbert S. Winokur Jr. (Houston, February 1, 2002). Our analysis here is based on the Powers Report and press reports and the analysis thereof in George J. Benston and Al L. Hartgraves, "Enron: What Happened and What We Can Learn from It," *Journal of Accounting and Public Policy*, vol. 21, no. 2 (2002), pp. 105–27.

11. SPEs may take the legal form of a partnership, corporation, trust, or joint venture.

12. For a complete description of the accounting rules governing consolidation of SPEs and other investments, see Benston and Hartgraves, "The Evolving Accounting Standards for Special Purpose Entities (SPEs) and Consolidations," *Accounting Horizons*, vol. 16, no. 3 (2002), pp. 245–58.

13. Summaries can be found in Benston and Hartgraves. More detailed descriptions appear in the Powers Report (2002).

14. This rule is set out in the FASB's Accounting for Contingencies (Financial Accounting Statement 5).

15. The FASB requirement is SFAS 57; the SEC requirement is contained in Regulation S-X item 404.

16. Charles W. Mulford and Eugene E. Comiskey, *The Financial Numbers Game: Detecting Creative Accounting Practices* (John Wiley & Sons, 2002).

17. The problems relating to misstatement of revenue have also been documented by Thomas Weirich, "Analysis of SEC Accounting and Auditing Enforcement Releases," *The Panel on Audit Effectiveness Report and Recommendations*, prepared for the Public Oversight Board (Washington, 2000), appendix F, pp. 223–28. This study examined the SEC's Accounting and Auditing Enforcement Releases (AAERs), which announce the results of investigations into audits of registrant corporations, issued between July 1, 1997, and December 31, 1999. Of the 96 AAERs issued against the Big Five audit firms and their clients, 68 percent involved the misstatement of revenue and accounts receivable.

18. Mark S. Beasley, Joseph V. Carcello, and Dana R. Hermanson, *Fraudulent Financial Reporting: 1987–1997: An Analysis of Public Companies* (Jersey City, N.J.: American Institute of Certified Public Accountants, 1999). The study was commissioned by the Committee of Sponsoring Organizations of the Treadway Commission. It is possible that the AAERs may not be fully representative of the SEC's enforcement activities, since the companies in the database reflect only a subset of all accounting and auditing problems.

19. An overlapping 50 percent overstated assets, 18 percent understated expenses and liabilities, and 12 percent misappropriated assets.

20. Financial Executives International, "Quantitative Measures of the Quality of Financial Reporting" (Morristown, N.J.: FEI Research Foundation, 2001). Powerpoint presentations (www.fei.org).

21. If the "not-available" observations are included in the group with market values under $500 million, the "small" corporations are 89 percent of the total in 1977–94; 79 percent in 1995–2000.

22. Zoe-Vonna Palmrose and Susan Scholz, "The Circumstances and Legal Consequences of Non-GAAP Reporting: Evidence from Restatements," Contemporary Accounting Research Conference, held in Ontario, Nov. 2–3, 2002, and sponsored by CGA-Canada Research Foundation and the Canadian Institute of Chartered Accountants.

23. For one analysis of the costs of the corporate disclosure crisis of 2002, see Carol Graham, Robert Litan, and Sandip Sukhtankar, "Cooking the Books: The Cost to the Economy," Brookings Policy Brief 106, July 2002.

24. In the 1998–2000 period, 24 percent of the restatements resulted from enforcement actions by the SEC; compared with 16 percent in the 1990–97 period. For an entertaining and insightful account of the SEC's actions during this period, it is best to go to the source, Arthur Levitt himself. See Arthur Levitt with Paula Dwyer, *Take on the Street: What Wall Street and Corporate America Don't Want You to Know. What You Can Do to Fight Back* (Pantheon Books, 2002).

25. The increased use of options to compensate senior managers appears to have been driven, at least in part, by the 1993 tax law, which limits the deductibility of cash compensation over $1 million unless it is "performance based."

26. For a theoretical analysis in line with the speculations we offer here, see Lucian Bebchuk, Jesse Fried, and David Walker, "Managerial Power and Rent Extraction in the Design of Executive Compensation," *University of Chicago Law Review*, vol. 69, no. 3 (Summer 2002), pp. 751–846.

27. For perhaps one of the strongest critiques of the excesses in corporate compensation, and the misuse of stock options in particular, by a leading business organization, the Conference Board, see the report of its Blue Ribbon Commission on Public Trust and Private Enterprise, September 17, 2002 (www.conference-board.org/knowledge/governCommission.cfm).

28. Currently, GAAP allows firms to recognize stock options as an expense when they are exercised, which is determined by the grantee. U.S. income tax law, however, actually *requires* expensing of options at the time they are exercised.

29. Fischer Black and Myron Scholes, "The Pricing of Options and Corporate Liabilities," *Journal of Political Economy*, vol. 81, no. 3 (1973), pp. 637–54. The authors of this article, together with Robert Merton, received the Nobel Prize in Economics in 1997 largely because of the development of this formula for valuing stock options.

30. In particular, the formula assumes that past variation in stock prices is a good guide to the future, and that whatever interest rate is chosen is constant during the term of the option.

31. "Special Report: The Angry Market," *Business Week*, July 29, 2002, p. 45. A Merrill Lynch analysis suggested that the negative earnings impact from expensing stock options could range from as little as 2 percent in the energy industry to as much as 39 percent in information technology. See Lina Saigol, "Investment Banks Feel The Growing Pressure to Treat Stock Options as Expense," *Financial Times*, August 8, 2002, p. 17.

32. Thus, although we agree with the requirement to expense stock options that would have resulted under legislation offered by Senator John C. McCain in 2002 (voted down in the Senate), we side with those who opposed the bill on process grounds, namely, that Congress should not be engaged in the setting of accounting standards. At the same time, we are not opposed to a congressional mandate that the FASB study the issue, a proposal offered by Senator Carl Levin that was affirmed by the Senate shortly thereafter and included in the final version of Sarbanes-Oxley.

33. John M. Foster and Wayne S. Upton, "Understanding the Issues: Measuring Fair Value," vol. 3 (FASB, June 2001), p. 4.

34. AICPA, *Investment Company Guide* (section 1.32).

35. FASB Financial Accounting Standard (SFAS) 115.

36. If adopted, for fiscal years beginning after December 15, 2003, the AICPA-ACSEC Proposed Statement of Position entitled *Clarification of the Scope of the Audit and Accounting Guide Audits of Investment Companies and Equity Method Investors for Investment in Investment Companies* would prohibit the procedure described in the text. This statement essentially would restrict investment company fair-value accounting to registered investment companies and legally and actually separate investment companies, no owner of which owns 20 percent or more of its financial interests. This December 17, 2002, "Exposure Draft" was cleared by the FASB and, if adopted, would become part of GAAP.

37. A reader of our draft asked how we would account for "instruments, such as certain derivatives, for which there is no measurement attribute other than fair value." First, in accordance with the conservative bias in accounting and consistent with accounting for nontraded securities generally, gains on derivatives for which market quotations are not available should not be reported as income. Second, estimated losses on derivatives should be reported, as are estimated losses generally. We do not understand why derivatives for which market quotations are not available should be treated differently from other assets or liabilities. Indeed, when derivatives are used for hedging (as is usually the situation for most companies), the measurement is less of a problem because the gains and losses tend to be offset.

38. Coffee cites and discusses two cases. The first is *Lampf, Pleva, Lipkind & Petigrow v. Gilbertson*, 501 U.S. 350, 359–61 (1991), which created a federal rule requiring plaintiffs to file suit within one year of when they should have known of the violation underlying their action, but in no event more than three years after the violation; previously the state-law-based rule allowed suits to be filed from five to six years after the alleged violation. The second case is *Central Bank of Denver, N.A. v. First Interstate of Denver, N.A.*, 511 U.S. 164 (1994), which eliminated private "aiding and abetting" liability in securities fraud cases.

39. John P. Coffee Jr., "Understanding Enron: 'It's about the Gatekeepers, Stupid,'" Draft paper, Columbia Law School, 2002, p. 13. Coffee advances a similar argument in his unpublished manuscript, "What Caused Enron? A Short Legal and Economic History of the 1990's," paper presented at the Wharton Impact Conference called "New American Rules for Business? Post-Scandal Directions for Policy and Governance," held October 17–18, 2002, in Philadelphia.

40. In particular, the law assigns joint and several liability only where the jury specifically finds that the defendant knowingly violated the securities laws.

41. Dan Carney, "Don't Toss This Stock-Fraud Law. Just Fix It," *Business Week*, August 5, 2002, p. 86.

42. David S. Hilzenrath, "SEC Seeks Reform of Auditor Controls; Battered Enron Fires Accounting Firm," *Washington Post*, January 18, 2002, p. A1.

43. Similarly, the German equivalent to the AICPA, the Wirtschafts-prüferkammer or WPK, mounts disciplinary proceedings against wayward accountants, referring serious cases to prosecutors. However, even the few cases that have been prosecuted have resulted in very light penalties—warnings or relatively small fines (pursuant to a reprimand).

44. Hilzenrath, "SEC Seeks Reform of Auditor Controls." See also David S. Hilzenrath, "Pitt Seeks Closer Watch on Auditors," *Washington Post*, December 12, 2001, p. E1.

45. Sarbanes-Oxley Act of 2002 (§101).

46. The evolution of the FASB's actions (or inactions) are traced in the source cited in note 12.

47. Mike McNamee, "FASB: Rewriting the Book on Bookkeeping," *Business Week*, May 20, 2002, pp. 123–24. See also Dennis Beresford, "It's Time to Simplify Accounting Standards," *Journal of Accountancy* (March 1999), pp. 65–67, who makes a similar recommendation.

48. The United States is not the only country where politics has infected the accounting standards-setting process. The same has happened in Australia. See Stephen A. Zeff, "'Political' Lobbying on Proposed Standards: A Challenge to the IASB," *Accounting Horizons*, vol. 16 (March 2002), pp. 43–54.

49. Of course, if large institutional investors were more organized, we would be less concerned about unbalanced political influence in standard setting. But until this happens, we believe the point made in the text remains valid.

Chapter Three

1. New York Stock Exchange Corporate Accountability and Listing Standards Committee, "NYSE Proposals," June 6, 2002. NASDAQ, "Proposed Rule Changes—Corporate Governance Proposals," November 20, 2002. Available at www.nasdaq.com/about/proposedrulechanges.stm.

2. For a thorough review suggesting that the movement is more than window dressing, see Louis Lavelle, "The Best & Worst Boards: How the Corporate Scandals are Sparking a Revolution in Governance," *Business Week*, October 7, 2002, pp. 104–14.

3. The most prominent supporters of this idea are the last two chief accountants of the SEC, Lynn Turner and Robert Herdman.

4. Furthermore, the Sarbanes-Oxley Act calls for a General Accounting Office study of rules-based vs. principles-based accounting standards.

5. See, for example, Dennis Beresford, "Accounting and Investor Protection Issues Raised by Enron and Other Public Companies," testimony before the Senate Banking Committee, 107 Cong. 2 sess., February 26, 2002.

6. *McKinsey Global Investor Opinion Survey on Corporate Governance*, July 2002 (www.mckinsey.com/governance).

7. "The Hunt for Liquidity," *Economist*, July 28, 2001, p. 65.

8. William L. Griever, Gary A. Lee, and Francis E. Warnock, "The U.S. System for Measuring Cross-Border Investment in Securities: A Primer with a Discussion of Recent Developments," *Federal Reserve Bulletin*, October 2001, pp. 633–40.

9. A depository receipt is a negotiable instrument backed by the shares of the foreign firm, which are typically placed in a trust with a local (U.S. or European) bank.

10. Stijn Claessens, Daniela Klingbiel, and Sergio L. Schmukler, "The Future of Stock Markets in Emerging Markets: Evolution and Prospects," *Brookings-Wharton Papers on Financial Services* (forthcoming).

11. In addition to the sharp rise of cross-border flows of portfolio capital, flows of more permanent equity (foreign direct investment), as well as debt capital (bonds and bank loans), also have risen sharply over the past several decades, faster than the growth of trade in goods and services (and faster than gross domestic product). For one guide to the data, see Ralph C. Bryant, *Turbulent Waters: Cross-Border Finance and International Governance* (Brookings, forthcoming). See

also Benn Steil, *Why Integrate The Transatlantic Secondary Markets?* (New York: Council on Foreign Relations, forthcoming).

12. Linda Tesar and Ingrid Werner, "The Internationalization of Securities Markets since the 1987 Crash," *Brookings-Wharton Papers on Financial Services* (1998), pp. 281–349. For an excellent summary of the literature on home-country bias, see Karen K. Lewis, "Trying to Explain Home BIFRS in Equities and Consumption," *Journal of Economic Literature*, vol. 37 (1999), pp. 571–608.

13. We, of course, have already argued that the main failure in Enron was the failure of the company to adhere to the existing GAAP standard. However, a detailed study by the Examiner in Bankruptcy has revealed that Enron's managers, with the aid of bankers and possibly its auditor, used technical compliance with an aggressive application of GAAP rules to avoid the substance of those rules. These actions enabled Enron to avoid reporting substantial amounts of debt, while inflating its net income and enhancing its reported cash flows from operations. See "First Interim Report of Neal Batson, Court-Appointed Examiner, United States Bankruptcy Court, Southern District of New York, In Re: Enron Corp. Et al., Debtors, September 21, 2002."

14. Others have also urged more competition among standard setters. See, for example, Ronald A. Dye and Shyam Sunder, "Why Not Allow FASB and IASB Standards to Compete in the U.S.," *Accounting Horizons*, vol. 15, no. 3 (September 2001), pp. 257–71.

15. Benn Steil, *Building a Transatlantic Securities Market* (New York: Council on Foreign Relations, 2002).

16. Steil, *Building a Transatlantic Securities Market.* The main virtue claimed for exchange competition is lower trading costs. But Steil also suggests that competition in disclosure regimes would encourage more disclosure.

17. Another possible objection to allowing mutual recognition of exchanges is that it could expose smaller, less sophisticated investors to greater risks (if the foreign exchanges so recognized did in fact contain higher-risk stocks, with less transparent or effective corporate governance rules than may apply in the home country). If this objection were valid, it could be satisfied by restricting access to foreign exchanges doing business in a home country only to institutions and wealthy, sophisticated individuals.

18. One potential debate we do not resolve here is whether it might also be desirable for policymakers to promote industry-specific standards and the bodies that issue them. This would further promote competition, without necessarily entailing a loss in transparency. That is because apples-to-apples comparisons across industries may not be as important to promoting transparency as more standardized reporting that permits better comparisons of firms within the same industry.

19. Roughly a month before Congress created the oversight board, the SEC proposed its own version of the idea, but its proposal was overtaken by events after WorldCom's earnings restatement came to light. From that time forward, consensus quickly developed within Congress that only a statutorily authorized body would have the requisite legal clout and authority to oversee the auditing profession properly.

20. Congress ultimately appropriated $573 million for the SEC in fiscal year 2003, roughly $100 million more than the agency received the previous year, but about $200 million short of the figure that Congress had authorized earlier in the year. For a review of the challenges confronting the SEC, see Megan Barnett, "Oh, To Slay a Dragon," *U.S. News & World Report*, October 21, 2002, pp. 40–42.

21. See, for example, Kirstin Downey Grimsley, "Signing the Bottom Line: Top Executives at 16 companies Certify Their Books," *Washington Post*, August 1, 2002, p. E1. One study has found that the fact that CEOs did or did not sign made no significant difference to the share prices of their companies. See *The Economist*, September 28, 2002, p. 60.

22. Shareholder approval of executive compensation packages has also been introduced in some companies in Great Britain.

23. See www.nasdaqnews.com and www.nyse.com.

24. A preliminary assessment in 2001 by the SEC found that for publicly held firms surveyed, nonaudit fees accounted for about three-fourths of the revenue earned by auditing firms. However, fees related to tax preparation and advice (which often are substantial) are included in "nonaudit fees" and are not precluded by legislation or in practice. See David S. Hilzenrath, "Opening The Books on Corporate Auditors: Report Shows Audit Fees Reflect a Fraction of the Business Accountants Do With Firms They Review," *Washington Post*, June 3, 2001, p. H1.

25. It has been claimed that the entry of audit firms to consulting distorted the culture of the firms away from audit quality and solely toward growth and profitability. For example, see the article on the demise of Andersen by John A. Byrne, "John Berardino's Fall From Grace," *Business Week*, August 12, 2002, pp. 51–56. This critique ignores the fact that the partners in firms such as Andersen, if driven primarily by revenue growth and profitability, could have embarked on an aggressive campaign to capture audit business and compromised audit quality just the same.

26. A less far-reaching measure, which the SEC was considering at the time this book went to press, would be to ban accounting firms from directly basing their auditors' compensation on the volume of consulting services provided to particular clients. This proposal would directly address the adverse incentive problems created by auditors engaging in non-audit work without banning the provision of the two to the same client. See David S. Hilzenrath, "Auditors May Face Curbs on Incentives," *Washington Post*, November 19, 2002, p. E1.

27. The idea of shifting the hiring and firing of auditors to insurers was initially proposed, to the best of our knowledge, by Joshua Ronen, "A Market Solution to the Accounting Crisis," *New York Times*, March 8, 2002, p. A21.

Chapter Four

1. Management decisions can also adversely affect the value of intangible assets even as current earning may be increased. For example, in deciding to cut back on the number of employees, advertising, or research and development efforts, corporate leaders may save money in the short run and thereby increase reported earnings (or reduce reported losses). However, these "economies" could also significantly diminish the value of intangible assets, by harming employee morale, eroding customer demand, and reducing the number and quality of innovations.

2. Baruch Lev, *Intangibles: Management, Measurements, and Reporting* (Brookings, 2001), pp. 8–9. See also Jonathan Law and Pam Cohen Kalafut, *Invisible Advantage: How Intangibles Are Driving Business Performance* (Cambridge, Mass.: Perseus Publishing, 2002).

3. This is equivalent to saying that the market is estimating the present value of higher future net cash flows than were reported in the previous period, which could be shown as assets if accountants were able to calculate trustworthy present values. For more formal analyses of the sources of intangible value, especially among high-tech companies, see Robert Hall, "E-Capital: The Link between the Labor Market and the Stock Market in the 1990s," *Brookings Papers on Economic Activity, 2: 2000*, pp. 73–118; and Erik Brynjolfsson, Lorin M. Hitt, and Shinkyu Yang, "Intangible Assets: Computers and Organizational Capital," *Brookings Papers on Economic Activity, 1: 2002*, pp. 137–81.

4. The acronym stands for Extensible Business Reporting Language, which is based on Extensible Markup Language (XML), the successor to the original language of the Internet, HTML (or Hyper Text Markup Language). For a guide to XBRL, see the website maintained by its sponsors (www.xbrl.org), as well as an excellent chapter on the subject in Samuel A. DiPiazza Jr. and Robert G. Eccles, *Building Public Trust: The Future of Corporate Reporting* (John Wiley & Sons, 2002), pp. 129–52.

5. See www.accounting.rutgers.edu/raw/aicpa/ackn.htm, sections 3.7 and 3.13.

6. DiPiazza and Eccles, *Building Public Trust*.

7. OECD, "Public-Private Forum on Value Creation in the Knowledge Economy—Overview," 2000 (www.oecd.org/daf/corporateaffairs/disclosure/inangibles.htm).

8. For other discussions, see Andrew Lymer, ed., "Special Section: The Internet and Corporate Reporting in Europe," *European Accounting Review,* vol. 8, no. 2 (1999), pp. 287–396; FASB, *Business Reporting Research Project: Electronic Distribution of Business Reporting Information,* 2000 (www.fasb.org); and Robert E. Litan and Peter J. Wallison, *The GAAP Gap: Corporate Disclosure in the Internet Age* (Washington: AEI-Brookings Joint Center for Regulatory Studies, 2000).

9. Of course, even with more frequent reports, firms may still find ways to manage annual or even quarterly earnings, to the extent investors put value in the reports. One common technique is to count otherwise extraordinary sales of assets as routine transactions conducted in the course of regular business. Several large companies apparently resorted to this practice in late 2002, even after all of the publicity associated with the accounting scandals earlier that year. For an illustrative guide, see David Henry and Heather Timmons, "Still Spinning Numbers," *Business Week,* November 11, 2002, pp. 120–21.

10. There is no guarantee of its success. XBRL, after all, is being developed by a consortium of companies, each with its own interests. The more companies that participate, the wider the usage of XBRL, but then the more unwieldy its governance structure becomes. For this reason, some analysts believe that standards are best developed on a proprietary basis, by a single company with a strong profit motive in the outcome—the best example being Microsoft's operating system for personal computers. However, the development of HTML and XML, the two key languages on the Internet, serves as a strong counterexample to the proprietary view. Similarly, the growing success of the "open source" movement in operating systems also is strong evidence that cooperative ventures can produce successful standards. One such effort, announced in August 2002 by NASDAQ, Microsoft, and PricewaterhouseCoopers, consists of a pilot program to give investors access to financial information in XBRL for twenty-one NASDAQ-listed companies. See www.nasdaq.com/xbrl.

11. This bias has also been documented in the academic literature. See Leslie Boni and Kent Womack, "Wall Street's Credibility Problem: Misaligned Incentives and Dubious Fixes?" *Brookings-Wharton Papers on Financial Services* (Brookings, 2002), pp. 93–130.

12. As it is now, investors can obtain independent research reports if they want to; in any event, with the spread of Internet technology, this will become even easier than in the past.

Notes to Appendix

1. For more detailed comparisons see, for example, Carrie Bloomer, ed., *The IASC-U.S. Comparison Project: A Report on the Similarities and Differences between*

NOTES TO PAGES 96–101

IASC Standards and U.S. GAAP. Based on a Study Undertaken by the FASB Staff. 2d ed. (Norwalk, Conn.: Financial Accounting Standards Board, 1999); and David Cook, and others, eds., *IAS/US GAAP Comparison* (London: Ernst and Young, 2000).

2. Some U.S. GAAP standards use a principles-based approach. One of them is SFAS 5, Accounting for Contingencies. FASB staff conducted a survey of seventy-five U.S. accounting experts, asking them to rate the best and worst U.S. GAAP standards. SFAS 5 was rated the third-best standard, in part because it is "not too complicated and provides general guidelines, requiring reasonable management judgment, [is] applicable to many different types of economic events, [. . . and] is operational and has not required much maintenance by the FASB." See Cheri L. Reither, "What Are the Best and the Worst Accounting Standards?" *Accounting Horizons,* vol. 12, no. 3 (September 1998), pp. 283–92.

3. In IFRS there is a limited overriding rule that allows a company to deviate from an individual rule if that would result in misleading financial statements in "extremely rare circumstances." This broad rule is borrowed from U.K. GAAP and has an analogue in the EU accounting directives. While a similar provision is included in the Code of Conduct of the American Institute of Certified Public Accountants, deviations from U.S. GAAP have been almost nonexistent, even though the situation would seem to arise more often in a rules-based system.

4. Lease accounting has been under discussion because the current distinction between capital and operating leases does not capture the "gray" area of lease contracts but does offer much leeway for earnings management.

5. If the proposal to restrict investment company fair-value accounting to legitimate investment companies is adopted, this procedure will no longer be permitted under U.S. GAAP after December 15, 2003. See chapter 3, note 36.

6. See IASB, "Exposure Draft of Proposed Amendments to IAS 32, Financial Instruments: Disclosure and Presentation" and "IAS 39, Financial Instruments: Recognition and Measurement," June 2002.

Contributors

GEORGE J. BENSTON is John H. Harland Professor of Finance, Accounting, and Economics at the Goizueta Business School and professor of economics at the college, Emory University.

MICHAEL BROMWICH is CIMA Professor of Accounting and Financial Management at the London School of Economics.

ROBERT E. LITAN is vice president and director of Economic Studies at the Brookings Institution, where he also holds the Cabot Family Chair in Economics.

ALFRED WAGENHOFER is professor of management accounting and control at the University of Graz, Austria, and professor at the European Institute for Advanced Studies in Management, Brussels.

Index

Accounting abuses: difficulty of proving fraud by CEOs, 69; studies of, 30–35; types of, 30–31. *See also* Enron

Accounting and auditing enforcement releases (AAERs), 31–32

Accounting firms. *See* Arthur Andersen; Auditing and auditors

"Agency" function of accounting, 20

AICPA. *See* American Institute of Certified Public Accountants

American Institute of Certified Public Accountants (AICPA): failure of enforcement by, 43–44; on fair value accounting, 39; function of, 21, 23; self-interest problems of, 66; XBRL creation by, 89

Arthur Andersen: consulting business of, 72; failure as auditor, 2, 66; liability for litigation, 72; litigation against, 43; role

in Enron scandal, 2, 24, 26, 28, 29–30, 58; sanctioning of, 2, 45; and SPE accounting by Enron, 51, 58

Assets: fair value of, 38–41; overstatement of, 31. *See also* Intangible assets; Valuation

Audit committees. *See* Board of directors

Auditing and auditors: costs of scandals for, 34; discipline for violations, 45–46; ethical and professional standards needed for, 77; external auditors, role of, 21, 23, 85; and fair-value accounting, 40; incentives for accurate auditing, 13, 71–72; increasing costs of audits for clients, 13, 73–74; individual auditor responsibility, 45, 72; liability of auditors, 42, 72; litigation against auditors, 33, 42; nonaudit business restrictions, 13, 72–73; partner misconduct, reasons

JOINT CENTER

AEI-BROOKINGS JOINT CENTER FOR REGULATORY STUDIES

Director
Robert W. Hahn

Codirector
Robert E. Litan

Fellows
Robert W. Crandall
Christopher C. DeMuth
Randall W. Lutter
Clifford M. Winston

In response to growing concerns about the impact of regulation on consumers, business, and government, the American Enterprise Institute and the Brookings Institution established the AEI-Brookings Joint Center for Regulatory Studies. The primary purpose of the center is to hold lawmakers and regulators more accountable by providing thoughtful, objective analysis of existing regulatory programs and new regulatory proposals. The Joint Center builds on AEI's and Brookings's impressive body of work over the past three decades that evaluated the economic impact of regulation and offered constructive suggestions for implementing reforms to enhance productivity and consumer welfare. The views in Joint Center publications are those of the authors and do not necessarily reflect the views of the staff, council of academic advisers, or fellows.